## DATE DUE

| | | | |
|---|---|---|---|
| | | | |
| | | | |
| | | | |
| | | | |
| | | | |
| | | | |
| | | | |
| | | | |
| | | | |
| | | | |
| | | | |
| | | | |
| | | | |
| | | | |
| | | | |
| | | | |
| | | | |
| | | | |
| | | | PRINTED IN U.S.A. |

# ANXIETY

## Biographies of Disease Series

Stroke
*Jonathan A. Edlow*

Autism
*Lisa D. Benaron*

Rabies
*P. Dileep Kumar*

Influenza
*Roni K. Devlin*

ADHD
*Paul Graves Hammerness*

Food Allergies
*Alice C. Richer*

Anorexia
*Stacy Beller Stryer*

Obesity
*Kathleen Y. Wolin, Sc.D., and Jennifer M. Petrelli*

Sports Injuries
*Jennifer A. Baima*

Polio
*Daniel J. Wilson*

Cancer
*Susan Elaine Pories, Marsha A. Moses, and Margaret M. Lotz*

Fibromyalgia
*Kim D. Jones and Janice H. Hoffman*

Alcoholism
*Maria Gifford*

# ANXIETY

## Cheryl Winning Ghinassi

Biographies of Disease
*Julie K. Silver, M.D., Series Editor*

 ABC-CLIO

Santa Barbara, California • Denver, Colorado • Oxford, England

**Library of Congress Cataloging-in-Publication Data**

Ghinassi, Cheryl Winning.
  Anxiety / Cheryl Winning Ghinassi.
    p. cm. — (Biographies of disease)
  Includes bibliographical references and index.
    ISBN 978-0-313-36242-2 (hard copy : alk. paper) — ISBN 978-0-313-36243-9
(ebook) 1. Anxiety disorders—Popular works. I. Title.
  RC531.G475  2010
  616.85′22—dc22      2010000097

ISBN:  978-0-313-36242-2
EISBN: 978-0-313-36243-9

14  13  12  11  10    1  2  3  4  5

This book is also available on the World Wide Web as an eBook.
Visit www.abc-clio.com for details.

Greenwood
An Imprint of ABC-CLIO, LLC

ABC-CLIO, LLC
130 Cremona Drive, P.O. Box 1911
Santa Barbara, California 93116-1911

This book is printed on acid-free paper (∞)

Manufactured in the United States of America

I dedicate this book to my daughter, Rose, and to my parents,
James and Edith Winning.

# Contents

# Series Foreword

E very disease has a story to tell: about how it started long ago and began to disable or even take the lives of its innocent victims, about the way it hurts us, and about how we are trying to stop it.

In this Biographies of Disease series, the authors tell the stories of the diseases that we have come to know and dread. The stories of these diseases have all of the components that make for great literature. There is incredible drama played out in real-life scenes from the past, present, and future. You'll read about how men and women of science stumbled trying to save the lives of those they aimed to protect. Turn the pages and you'll also learn about the amazing success of those who fought for health and won, often saving thousands of lives in the process. If you don't want to be a health professional or research scientist now, when you finish this book you may think differently. The men and women in this book are heroes who often risked their own lives to save or improve ours. This is the biography of a disease, but it is also the story of real people who made incredible sacrifices to stop it in its tracks.

Julie K. Silver, M.D.
Assistant Professor, Harvard Medical School
Department of Physical Medicine and Rehabilitation

# Preface

M ost people can relate to anxiety disorders more easily than to any other mental health disorder. We all experience anxiety and stress; these feelings are a natural part of our functioning. Each of us exists somewhere on a spectrum of anxiety vulnerability, which ranges from a zone of appropriate response to true anxiety-provoking events to a psychobiological medical disorder known as an anxiety disorder.

As a psychologist, I encounter the full spectrum of these responses in my clinical practice. People enter therapy to deal with life stresses, anxiety reactions to life events, and full-blown, diagnosable anxiety disorders. I see people who suffer from a mixture of depression and anxiety and people who have an anxiety disorder in addition to another major mental illness. I see anxiety disorders, more often than any other disorder, present in my own family, friends, and acquaintances. Anxiety disorders are prevalent throughout the world's population (an estimated 29 percent of all adults in the United States have had an anxiety disorder in their lifetime), and we speak of "life's anxieties," "cultural anxiety," and "times of anxiety" in our day-to-day life. Anxiety is an interesting topic indeed.

This book begins by looking at the phenomenon of anxiety both as a normal part of life and as a medical disorder, because the two experiences of anxiety are linked. The major focus, however, is on the medical disorders of anxiety. We humans have had various conceptualizations of anxiety disorders and their treatment over the course of our history. Chapters 2 and 3 present the story of how we have tried to make sense of these disorders, leading to the explosion of knowledge in the last half century. Even in my own career, which spans a mere thirty years, I have seen conceptualizations and treatments evolve.

Chapter 4 briefly describes the various anxiety disorders; presents research on genetics, models of etiology, and statistics showing the prevalence of anxiety disorders in the population (epidemiology); and provides information on cultural aspects of anxiety disorders. When I educate patients about the biological and genetic bases of anxiety disorders, they are often surprised and greatly relieved. I often hear comments such as, "Oh yeah, my grandmother, she was really really nervous" and "You mean I'm not crazy?" Despite the proliferation of available information, particularly on the Web, many people still hold to the view that their anxiety disorders are signs of psychological failings and weakness. Chapter 5 explores the neurobiology that underpins anxiety disorders. This is an area that has experienced tremendous growth, especially in the last thirty years, thanks to technological advances in biochemistry and neuroimaging.

Because anxiety disorders are medical disorders, they have specific diagnostic criteria. These are presented in Chapter 6, along with a discussion of the elements of a comprehensive clinical assessment. Patients' cases are used to illustrate the various symptom presentations of the anxiety disorders. We follow these patients into Chapter 7 to highlight the treatment of the specific disorders. I find satisfaction in treating people with anxiety disorders, as I am able to provide patients with tools to manage their disorders, and yet I still find a challenge in understanding the unique experiences and nuances of each person's case. Many patients are able to come to understand and manage their anxiety disorders and have a better quality of life.

The final chapter picks up all the threads introduced earlier—conceptualization, classification (diagnosis), biology and genetics, and treatment—and looks at the future directions of research in these areas. We still have a journey ahead of us in understanding and treating anxiety disorders, but we have come so far. My hope is that the reader will gain an understanding of these disorders from both a medical and a human perspective.

I am indebted to my teachers in anxiety disorders, Dr. Steven Willis and Dr. Daniel Geller from Harvard Medical School and Dr. Richard Heimberg and Dr. David Barlow from my days at the State University of New York at Albany. Dr. Barlow's excellent book *Anxiety and Its Disorders: The Nature and*

*Treatment of Anxiety and Panic* provided much information for this text. My other teachers are my patients: children, adolescents, and adults who suffer from anxiety disorders. I continue to learn from them and feel honored to be part of their journeys to better health. My gratitude also goes to Elizabeth Davis Como, Dr. Julie Silver, and Dr. Kathleen Pajer, who contributed many useful comments on the manuscript, and to Kathleen Potter and Frances Sullivan for their unwavering support. I am grateful to my husband, Frank Ghinassi, who has inspired me to be persistent.

# 1

# Pictures of Anxiety

## SCENE 1

Dawn is still hours away in this prehistoric village situated in a mountainous forest region. A young man joins the departing hunting party for the second time. They slip quietly away from their village, heading into the forest near the river. In the dark, they proceed without sound. This young hunter has been taught by his elders how to walk silently and stealthily, and his training serves him well. He can smell the damp forest and feel the leaves of the lower branches lightly brush his face, and he is aware of every muscle fiber in his body. As the members of the party split up to begin their sweep of the area, the hunter's heart rate quickens and his breathing becomes more shallow and rapid. His eyes scan the forest in front of him, and his hearing seems especially acute. The hand grasping his bow is moist with sweat.

The young man feels confident and alert. He hopes that he will return with a magnificent buck that will feed and clothe his family well. He imagines the pride with which his father and mother will regard him. Suddenly, as he passes a large outcropping of rocks, he hears a rustling of leaves. Looking up, the hunter sees a mountain lion crouched above him. His heart pounds, and he cannot catch his breath. Although his hands and feet go cold, he feels a warm surge flush his upper body and face. His stomach lurches, he can hear the blood pulsing in his ears, and his mind races. Gone are his thoughts of glory and honor—instead, he envisions a horrible death in the forest. For an instant, he freezes.

A moment later, the hunter automatically leaps behind a huge boulder to the right of his pathway. His training comes back to him as he hears the words of his teachers. The muscle memory from repeated practice helps him respond. Moving fluidly, he steadies an arrow in his bow, and he takes aim as the mountain lion turns toward him. As the mighty cat pounces, the hunter releases the bowstring and hears the whistle of the arrow as it takes flight. The arrow meets its mark, and the mountain lion slumps to the ground. The young man stands poised for a moment, senses sharpened and heart still pounding. He cautiously approaches the fallen animal. Realizing that the mountain lion is dead, a wave of relief passes over him. He takes a deep breath of air, and his breathing slows. He can feel his heart rate slow down, and warmth returns to his hands and feet. All of a sudden, he feels enormously fatigued and weakened. He starts to tremble slightly and sits down on a nearby boulder. After a few minutes, his body returns to normal and his thinking shifts to the next tasks before him. The hunter signals his companions and prepares the cat for transport.

What you have just read is the experience of anxiety in two of its forms. As our young hunter walks through the woods and prepares for the hunt, his anxiety level has risen in the service of fine-tuning his performance. His senses are sharpened, and he is poised for action. His respiration changes to increase the oxygen flow to his brain and body to aid in thinking, sensing, and reacting. His heart rate increases, supplying his muscles with additional blood to enable quick, strong responses. As he becomes aware of imminent danger, a rush of adrenaline heightens his reactions and also redirects blood away from his stomach, creating nausea. This redirection of blood to certain organs and the large muscles prepares his body for fight or flight. Thinking is accelerated, allowing for rapid problem solving if he is not overwhelmed. In this situation, anxiety has saved the young hunter's life.

## SCENE 2

It is the end of the semester, and the week ahead is peppered with final exams. Kate is feeling stressed enough about her studies and realizes that her friends are avoiding her for reasons she can't comprehend. "Did I say something wrong? Did I forget something? Who did I tick off?" she thinks. Kate is trying to study, but she can't concentrate. "What is going to happen if they don't talk to me again tomorrow?" "Oh, no, I have this math exam and I just can't hold these theories in my head." She has lost her appetite, she's not sleeping well, and her stomach is in knots. "If I don't pull up my grade point average, my parents are going to kill me," she thinks.

This is also anxiety, the normal, everyday anxiety that we all experience from time to time. We worry and cannot escape the extraneous thoughts banging around in our brains. We can't eat (or we eat more); we can't sleep (or we sleep more). We are restless, tense, and jittery; we suffer from headaches and tightness in the chest. (Hmm, this also sounds like falling in love!) If we cannot control our anxiety and it becomes too intense, it can interfere with what we need to do. However, if we manage our anxiety, then it can motivate us to problem solve and put a plan into action.

## SCENE 3

Laura is driving to the grocery store to finish up her errands for the day. She needs to prepare dinner and make a few phone calls when she gets home. There is plenty of time to get things done, and for once she does not feel rushed. Suddenly, for no reason, she feels her heart pounding in her chest, and her chest feels tight. She starts to hyperventilate; her breathing becomes rapid and shallow, and she feels like she cannot get enough air. Her fingers begin to tingle and she trembles. Her face flushes red, her hands feel clammy, and she feels nauseous. "Oh no," she gasps. She thinks, "I must be having a heart attack. I've got to pull over." Managing to get the car to the side of the road, she sits there immobilized with fear. She is dizzy and feels as if she is not in her own body. Several minutes pass, and the symptoms begin to dissipate. Then, she feels drained and horrible. After being examined at the local emergency room, she is told that she has had a panic attack. In the following weeks, she grows reluctant to drive alone since she fears having another attack. Laura begins to have these attacks with some regularity.

Laura suffers from an anxiety disorder. Notice that her experience is not unlike that of the young hunter when confronted with the mountain lion. The significant difference is that Laura was not in any actual physical danger. She was not even experiencing everyday anxiety, as Kate was. In panic disorder, the panic attacks seem to come out of the blue. The physiological response is identical to the fight-or-flight response, but it has no appropriate trigger or cue. If she restricts her driving and limits her outings from home, she will suffer from agoraphobia as well. Panic disorder will significantly impair Laura's life.

## ANXIETY: NORMAL OR PATHOLOGICAL?

As we have seen, anxiety is a normal part of life. Anxiety presents on a continuum from relatively low-level anxiety, such as worry about tomorrow's exam, to midlevel anxiety, as we embark on a new experience such as the first day at a new school, to rather intense anxiety when we are faced with a major life problem. Anxiety is subjective; different people react at different levels relative to the concern at hand or to what they believe is at stake. We can be overwhelmed by anxiety or we can utilize it to heighten our performance. Anxiety can have its benefits.

### Anxiety as an Adaptive Survival Response

It has long been recognized and was elucidated by Charles Darwin that an organism's fight-or-flight reaction in response to an immediate threat serves the function of preserving the life of the individual. Darwin further suggests that the survival of the fittest occurs because of the inborn capacity to respond in such a manner. This enables the evolution of species. As one looks at the physiological changes that occur with the fight-or-flight response, it becomes clear that these changes are designed to do exactly that: preserve the individual's life. As we will discuss in more depth later, the changes that occur in the body all contribute to the mobilization of the organism to flee or stand and fight the threat. In addition, the more severe response of fainting, and its simultaneous drop in blood pressure, enables the animal or human to appear dead to a predator (not as useful to humans today as it was in prehistoric times). This response also reduces blood flow, thus minimizing blood loss in the event of an injury. Although we may no longer need to worry much about mountain lions, this response is still useful for avoiding harm, such as jumping out of the way of an oncoming car.

This discussion also leads us to make a distinction between anxiety and fear. Theorists such as Sigmund Freud and Søren Kierkegaard viewed *fear* as the response to a particular, observable threat and *anxiety* as undefined apprehension or anxiety without a particular stimulus or cue. We have since defined anxiety further, on the basis of the work of behavioral and cognitive psychologists. Clearly, we learn to be anxious when confronted by certain stimuli that have threatened us in the past. Also, because as humans we can analyze future situations, we can worry in advance about upcoming events. Therefore, anxiety is often related to specific stimuli.

### Anxiety as a Motivator to Problem Solving and Planning

In our thinking, we have moved beyond viewing anxiety as "objectless." Consequently, if there is an object of our anxiety and we are thinking individuals, can we not learn from this emotional response? Indeed we can. Howard Liddell, a psychologist working in the early part of the twentieth century, views anxiety as the "shadow of intelligence." Drawing from his research, he concludes that animals learn to be vigilant to future threats on the basis of their experience with the past threats. Liddell sees this as a parallel to human anxiety and worry, which promotes planning for the future. Because humans anticipate and prepare for future events, neural changes occur in our brains that foster intellectual and skill development.

We live this in our own lives over and over again. If we are anxious about a presentation, we gather information, rehearse, and learn our material. Facing a major sports competition, we hone our skills and practice.

At the end of the month is the first round of playoffs for the state championship in swimming. When you think about the meet, your stomach knots. You know you do well in some events, but the freestyle is just not your strength. Because you wish to be uniform in your performance, you devise a plan to talk with your coach and to get in some extra practice time. This plan is carried out and, although you still feel anxious as the meet approaches, you feel more confident.

### Anxiety as an Enhancer of Performance

Because anxiety can also help us perform at our optimum levels, it is not a bad thing that you feel anxious as the swim meet begins. Many musicians, actors, athletes, and other performers talk about the preliminary anxiety (feeling "psyched") that propels them forward with great energy and the confidence that they are up to the performance. They actually cultivate and embrace that feeling of anxiety and excitement. A recent study examines the differences in emotional state between performers who reported being helped by the anxiety they experienced before a competition and those who reported being hindered by it. This study concludes that positive anxiety, accompanied with confidence, facilitated performance, whereas negative feelings and interpretations of anxiety debilitated performance.

In 1908, Robert M. Yerkes and John D. Dodson showed that moderate anxiety enhanced performance over the experience of no anxiety. They also found, as we would all conclude, that severe anxiety impeded performance. Much research over the years has supported their work.

As the swim meet begins and you feel your heart rate increase, your senses sharpen and your breathing speeds up. You know with confidence that you are at the top of your game.

### Anxiety as a Medical Disorder

Unfortunately, there is a flip side to the benefits of anxiety. Uncontrolled anxiety, such as the crippling stage fright that inhibits performers and myriad other diagnosable anxiety disorders, can severely disrupt a person's daily life and life goals.

**Disrupted Concert Tours**

It is not unusual for musicians to cancel tours or refuse to perform publicly because of anxiety symptoms. Barbra Streisand panicked when she forgot the lyrics of a song during a concert in New York's Central Park, and she was unable to perform in public again for twenty-seven years. Singer Carly Simon, who has been very open about her anxiety disorder, stuttered as a child and was always a reluctant performer. In 1981, she was immobilized by a panic attack during a performance and later collapsed at a subsequent show. After this event, it was many years before she gave another live concert. Today, Simon uses a blood pressure medication called Inderal that dampens the physiological symptoms of anxiety to help her perform. In 2007, the band the White Stripes cancelled its tour because of the severe anxiety of its backup singer and drummer, Meg White. Allegedly, the band posted the following statement on their Web site: "Meg White is suffering from acute anxiety and is unable to travel at this time. . . . We hate to let people down and are very sorry."

Freud observed anxiety as a common experience in normal individuals. As we have discussed, he acknowledged its purpose in signaling the presence of danger to aid the individual to respond defensively. However, he also recognized that anxiety could be self-defeating and maladaptive. He, and others before him, called this *neurotic anxiety*. Pathological or neurotic anxiety is intense, disturbing, paralyzing, and debilitating. On the basis of research and scientific thought, particularly during the twentieth century, we have come to recognize pathological anxiety as comprising a group of true medical disorders.

The experience of pathological anxiety comes in many forms. The symptoms range from broad, nagging worries about multiple topics to specific intense phobias, such as the fear of heights. Some people experience obsessions, which are defined as thoughts or concerns that get stuck in one's head with little relief. Individuals often respond to these obsessions by developing compulsions, which are ritualized behaviors that cannot easily be relinquished. For example, repeated, harsh hand washing is compulsive behavior in response to the fear of and obsession about germs. As we saw with Laura, some people suffer from panic attacks. These are a just a few of the many faces of anxiety.

Research over the years has yielded a categorization and labeling of anxiety symptoms. Particular clusters of symptoms tend to occur together. By dividing these anxiety disorders into diagnostic groups, we are better informed in the assessment and treatment of individuals who suffer from pathological anxiety.

## The *DSM-IV-TR* Anxiety Disorders

Panic disorder without agoraphobia
Panic disorder with agoraphobia
Agoraphobia without history of panic disorder
Specific phobia
Social phobia
Obsessive-compulsive disorder
Posttraumatic stress disorder
Acute stress disorder
Generalized anxiety disorder
Anxiety disorder due to a medical condition
Substance-induced anxiety disorder
Anxiety disorder not otherwise specified

Psychiatry and psychology utilize the *Diagnostic and Statistical Manual IV-TR* (*DSM-IV-TR*), which was synthesized after many years of research and is published by the American Psychiatric Association to guide in the diagnosis of mental disorders.

In the United States, anxiety disorders constitute the single largest mental health problem. Upwards of 60 million people in the United States are estimated to have suffered from an anxiety disorder at some point in their lives. Anxiety disorders are chronic medical conditions that seldom see a cure. Instead, patients must learn to manage these illnesses from psychological and physiological perspectives. Anxiety disorders have a tremendous personal impact on quality of life, health, substance abuse, relationships, parenting, and academic and career performance. In addition, there are huge societal costs in terms of lost productivity and health care expenses. Psychologists, physicians, and philosophers have been trying to figure out the best ways to understand and treat anxiety disorders in the hope of eliminating the human suffering brought on by these illnesses.

# 2

# Anxiety through the Ages: Prehistory to the 1800s

## PREHISTORIC AND ANCIENT CIVILIZATIONS

Since we now know that fear and anxiety involve brain biology, genetics, and evolution, we can conclude that these emotions have existed as long as there have been people. Very early evidence and historic writings, however, make little distinction between anxiety disorders and more severe mental illness. Consequently, the early history of anxiety disorders is very much part of the early history of all mental illness, as well as the beginning of psychology and psychiatry.

### Spiritual Theories

From Paleolithic times, humans have attempted treatments for those suffering from mental anguish and odd behaviors. A procedure called trephining was practiced, which entailed the boring of a hole in the back of the skull to relieve pressure on the head. This drastic procedure would undoubtedly have killed more victims than it cured. Archeologists have also uncovered evidence that those suffering from mental disorders wore amulets to help drive away evil spirits.

Early ideas about mental illness fell into the realm of the mystical. Primitive humans embraced spiritual theories to explain many of life's phenomena and to calm the anxieties of their difficult lives. An attempt to explain strange behavior is later seen in the writings of the ancient Babylonians, who flourished from 2000 to 500 BCE. The Babylonians, like the Persians, Egyptians, and Hindus, concluded that mental and physical maladies were a result of powerful gods who had been angered by the disobedient individual.

The earliest references to fear and anxiety come to us from ancient Egypt, Rome, and Greece. The Greek god Pan, the instigator of fear and anxiety, was an irritable and unpredictable satyr whose bellowing would terrify humans. His name is the root of the word *panic*. Priests, wizards, shamans, medicine men, and magicians were the early healers of mental and physical illness. With the perceptions that mental illness was either inflicted by a god because of one's transgressions or actual demonic possession, the goal of treatment was purification. Incantations to the deities were often the first steps utilized to free the victim from his or her affliction. Loud noises, foul odors, and bitter potions were used to help remove evil spirits. If these steps failed, healers resorted to flogging, shock, starvation, torture, or surgery. The theory behind treatment for possession was that the body must be made uninhabitable for the demon.

The early Chinese also built their theories about mental illness and its treatment around sorcery and magic. Records dating to the fourteenth century BCE attribute headaches and other "head disorders" to "malevolent agencies of the wind." The Chinese established a broad social welfare policy to care for the ill; they tended to have a much more humane approach than other cultures of the time and eventually shifted away from supernatural explanations about mental illness. The *Shan Hai Ching*, written in the fourth century BCE, listed twenty drugs and herbal remedies that could be used for treating anger, fear, and jealousy. Mental disorders were perceived as the result of an imbalance in the "vital elements of life," particularly an overabundance of angry emotions. Acupuncture was developed as a method to help restore this essential balance. The philosophy of Taoism stressed the importance of balancing the opposing forces of the world (*yin* and *yang*) and urged the individual to be part of the rhythm of the world's natural forces.

Archeological excavations in India have revealed the earliest indications of the practice of yoga. These drawings of yoga positions date to approximately 3000 BCE. The evolution of yoga centered on developing an inner focus that allows for deeper understanding by balancing the physical and spiritual worlds and body and mind through meditation, breathing, physical postures, and teachings. Good health, long life, and the development of wisdom are goals of yoga that were later incorporated into the traditions of Hinduism. In the twentieth century, yoga was adopted by Western cultures as a remedy for stress, anxiety, and depression.

### Anxiety and Fear in Warfare

The Greeks and Romans were acutely aware of the role of anxiety and fear in warfare. The Greek commander Xenophon wrote in approximately 500 BCE, "I am sure that not numbers or strength bring victory in war; but whichever army goes into battle stronger in its soul." Greek and Roman generals worked to instill moral character by toughening their troops with strict regimens and hardship. They stressed self-respect and camaraderie in order to reduce the likelihood of acts of cowardice.

Because it is recognized that combat has an effect on soldiers and can result in battle-related maladies, which we now call posttraumatic stress disorder, troops have been rotated out of combat areas for centuries. The Greek historian Herodotus (480 BCE) writes that Spartan commanders defending Thermopylae released the battle-weary soldiers who "had no heart for the fight and were unwilling to take their share of the danger." Even today, soldiers are pulled from the line when they become emotionally exhausted and vulnerable to their fears and anxieties.

Historians have discovered evidence that herbal remedies and intoxicating substances such as opium have been used, especially for soldiers, since before recorded history. In some cultures, the fear and anxiety generated by an upcoming battle were often quelled by the use of mind-altering substances. The Koyak and Wiros tribes of central Russia (ca. 2000 BCE) developed a drug from the *Amanita muscaria* mushroom that reduced fear and increased endurance when ingested by their warriors. During the Crusades, Christian soldiers encountered Muslim warriors called *hashashin* because of their use of the herb hashish to reduce fear and pain. Later, the Spaniard Juan Pizarro (ca. 1530) recorded that Inca warriors chewed coca leaves (the source of cocaine) before going into battle.

## THE GREEKS AND THE CLASSICAL AGE

The Classical Age (500–332 BCE) of Greece yielded dramatic advancements in science and medicine. The philosopher Thales (652–588 BCE) believed that all of human behavior could be explained by underlying scientific principles. Consequently, Greek scholars eventually theorized that illness did not originate from gods or demons but rather from natural processes in the body.

### The Sixth Century BCE

Around the sixth century BCE, institutions called temples were established in the peaceful countryside of Greece away from the stresses of city and family life to treat the mentally and physically ill. These country retreats emphasized good diet, massage, cleanliness, pleasant music, and comfort. In addition, the Greeks used sedative drugs to calm their patients. Unfortunately, if patients did not respond to this treatment, they could be chained and flogged to exorcise the possessing demon. Eventually, philosopher-scientists of the sixth century would denounce these punishments and eliminate exorcism as a route to general health. The sixth century BCE was a time of great intellectual development, and the belief in spiritual causes of mental illness became less popular.

Pythagoras (582–510 BCE) applied the mathematical principles of balance and ratio to all things in the universe, including mental health. He believed that the body was constituted of biological humors (fluids) that must be in balance for a person to be physically and mentally healthy. In some ways, science has come full circle, since we currently study imbalances of neurotransmitters, hormones, and other chemicals as the source of many mental disorders.

Besides humoral balance, Pythagoras also believed that mental health could be achieved when the opposing forces of love and hate, among other dichotomies, were in balance. The opposing rhythmic movements of life, such as inhaling and exhaling and sleep and wakefulness, must also be in order. The disequilibrium in the forces was believed to bring about psychic pain and impairment. Therapeutic approaches to anxiety today still incorporate the regulation of breathing as a strategy to manage anxiety and panic. Current research also shows that disturbances in the sleep cycle affect mood and anxiety levels.

Pythagoras was the first Greek thinker to identify the brain as the seat of intelligence and rationality and, therefore, the source of mental dysfunction. He proposed an interface between psychic health and the soul. He viewed the brain as the seat of the soul's rationality and the heart as the seat of the soul's irrationality, a duality we still speak of today. ("My head tells me to go; my heart wants me to stay.") When an individual was free of mental disturbance, the soul would be in good health.

### The Asclepians

In Greek mythology, Asclepius was the son of Apollo and was designated as the god of medicine. The cult that built up around him followed the teachings of Pythagoras and founded temple-based hospitals based on compassionate healing traditions. A stay at one of these temples provided relaxation and healthful living based on nutrition, exercise, and restful sleep. Priests provided suggestions for care of the soul (the beginning of psychotherapy) and sought to engender a positive attitude toward recovery. Warm baths and daily massages were regular practices.

Alcmaeon (557–491 BCE) was a follower of Pythagoras who took the study of mental functioning to a further level because of his scientific research that involved the dissection of the brain and the central nervous system. Identifying the connection between the sensory nerves and the brain, he furthered the move away from mystical explanations for aberrant behavior and mental illness. Incorporating the biological humor theory, he posited that cerebral metabolism relied on the balance of the humoral fluxes. With his knowledge of anatomy and concepts of homeostasis (balance), Alcmaeon laid the groundwork for much of the scientific theorizing and exploration that followed.

The son of an Asclepian priest on the Greek island of Kos became one of the most revered physicians of all time. Hippocrates, who lived from 460 to 367 BCE, merged the scientific method of clinical observation and the search for underlying principles with compassionate holistic care. He insisted on the careful observation of the patient to determine the source of disorder. Hippocrates established the tradition in Western medicine of relying on empirical (observable) evidence, fact gathering, case studies, and outcome-based treatments. He produced the first written case studies on depression and phobias.

Hippocrates believed that the brain was the source of thought, intellect, and emotion, and he promoted the study of mental functioning to a clinical science. He saw the brain as the source of both pleasant and negative emotions: happiness, joy, and pleasure, as well as sorrow, grief, and fear. "Madness, dread and fear, aimless anxieties, sleeplessness, inopportune mistakes, and absentmindedness" were identified by Hippocrates as originating from the brain when it is not in balance.

### The First Classification System for Mental Disorders

Hippocrates also initiated a classification system for mental disorders that provided the groundwork of today's classification system that is relied upon by behavioral health professions. The *Diagnostic and Statistical Manual of Mental Disorders, Fourth Edition, Text Revision (DSM-IV-TR)*, published in 2000 by the American Psychiatric Association, delineates the criteria and differentiating features of the mental and personality disorders. It is a dynamic endeavor that is continually being updated as new information and patterns are observed and verified.

Hippocrates and his colleagues at the Kos College of Medicine in Athens established a rationale for distinguishing mental disorders and aberrant behaviors. They differentiated what we know as Axis I disorders in the *DSM-IV-TR*

**Figure 2.1** The Greek physician Hippocrates produced the earliest known case studies on phobias and depression. (Courtesy of National Library of Medicine)

(mental disorders such as depression, anxiety, and schizophrenia) from the Axis II disorders, which include the dysfunctional personality styles, or temperaments, as the Greeks called them. They identified phobias and hysteria as the anxiety disorders. Hysteria was limited to females and was supposedly caused by a wandering uterus. Hippocrates and his colleagues delineated four essential personality temperaments based on four humors which are associated with the four elements of water, fire, earth, and air. The respective humors are phlegm, blood, black bile, and yellow bile. It was believed that the dominance of one humor over the others created a particular personality type, and that the imbalance of humors was believed to cause mental or physical illness.

The concept of diagnosis was a major leap forward in this new area of philosophy, called medicine. Its importance lies in the utility of connecting the treatment to the symptoms of the patient. Hippocrates and his colleagues developed specific treatment regimens for particular diagnoses. These treatments were based on their humoral theories and strove to attain balance to restore essential health.

The monumental contributions of Hippocrates established the sciences of medicine and psychiatry. He wrenched the search for knowledge about bodily and mental functioning out of the realm of religion and the supernatural. The influence of Hippocrates would dominate the next thousand years and then fall into disrepute, only to resurface in the Renaissance to underpin medicine and psychology as we know them today.

### Socrates, Plato, and Aristotle

Socrates (470–399 BCE) developed a style of thinking based on the questioning of established assumptions and the seeking of answers in observable phenomena and in underlying truths. Intelligence and reason dominated his conceptualization of mental health and dysfunction. Like Pythagoras, he believed that the soul and mind were interconnected. He insisted that people care for their souls, since the body and its basic needs could corrupt both the mind and the soul. According to Socrates, "raving, fear, disorderly passions, and folly are due to the body." Self-analysis, examining one's inner mental life to identify truth and reason, was seen as the pathway to a healthy mind. This concept was another building block in the development of modern psychotherapy. Through knowledge, one could combat the temptations of the physical passions. "Know thyself" was Socrates' directive to his followers who were striving for a pure and healthy mind and soul.

Plato (429–347 BCE) established an academy in 387 BCE that became a major seat of philosophical learning as the Classical Age drew to an end. Following the lead of Hippocrates and Socrates, Plato believed strongly in the treatment of the whole person and recognized the need to address temperament issues along with the mental disorder. Plato supported the treatment of the "head," meaning the mind, to aid in the treatment of physical disorders. This concept is currently being championed in modern medicine.

Although Plato believed that some mental pathology was caused by supernatural forces, he proposed that mental disorders could also result from internal sources. Plato believed that overwhelming, powerful emotions and conflicts between different components of the psyche could affect a person's behavior. He proposed that erroneous beliefs held by the patient were the source of extreme emotions, such as anxiety, and behaviors followed upon that belief system. Plato used education and rational discussions to alter a person's faulty beliefs, as we do today with cognitive-behavioral therapy.

Plato's student Aristotle (384–322 BCE) was more of a scientist than a philosopher. His areas of interest, which he pulled together into written treatises, were a compilation of the knowledge of his time. Aristotle was the first person to observe and record descriptions and stages of human development. Despite gathering evidence to the contrary, Aristotle accepted the notion that the heart, not the brain, was the center of emotion and thought. He wrote, "The brain is a residue, lacking any sensitive faculty." In his view, the heart was the center of the soul and was capable of integrating all the senses.

Although he dismissed the importance of the brain, Aristotle emphasized the value of sensory impressions in human behavior and learning. In addition, Aristotle identified the significance of associational linkages and the reinforcement of behavior as key avenues to learning. Associational linkages play a significant role in the development and maintenance of anxiety, fears, and phobias. Learning to be afraid of all dogs as a result of being bitten by one dog is an example of the role that associations play in development of a phobia.

## THE ROMAN EMPIRE

The Roman Empire (ca. 500 BCE to 325 CE), which overlapped and followed the Greek Classical Age, placed less emphasis on the development of psychology and medicine and relied on the previous teachings and theories of the Greeks. Nevertheless, several significant ideas did evolve during the Roman Empire. Aretaeus (30–90 CE) was the first physician to observe and record the long-term course of mental illness as he followed the lives of patients. He also studied premorbid (prior to illness) conditions that made patients vulnerable to the later development of a mental disorder.

Galen (131–201 CE) is another monumental figure in the science of medicine. He contributed significant information about neuroanatomy and viewed the nervous system as the key to mental functioning. Galen's major contribution was his compilation and interpretation of the accumulated knowledge of the Greeks and Romans. His categorization and description of mental disorders covered most of the disorders presented in the *DSM-IV-TR* today, including anxious depression and obsessionality.

Aurelianus (255–320) was a follower of Galen, but he unfortunately began a regressive movement back to the supernatural explanations of mental illness, which coincided with a general shift in thinking away from science as the Roman Empire began to decline and disintegrate. Along with the decline of science came the return of barbaric treatment for the mentally ill.

As Rome declined and Christianity became more ascendant, there was an even stronger pull toward the belief in demonic possession and the sin-based theories of earlier times. Treatment became increasingly moralistic and judgmental. The works of the Greek philosophers were banned, and strong anti-intellectualism took hold. Although some thinkers, such as St. Augustine

(354–430) and later the Jewish physician Maimonides (1135–1204), attempted to reconcile Greek philosophy with Christianity and with Jewish and Islamic law, respectively, the emphasis on spiritual explanations for mental maladies flourished. Europe slipped into the Dark Ages, and rational thinking and science waned for over a thousand years.

## THE MIDDLE AGES

The early Middle Ages, often referred to as the Dark Ages, began with the fall of the Roman Emperor Romulus Augustus in 476 and lasted until approximately 1000 CE. Epidemics, famine, pestilence, and chaos in the political and social order followed the disintegration of the Roman Empire and instilled fear and terror in the general populace. Scholars and commoners alike, rather than turning to rationality, looked to spirituality as an attempt to comprehend and control their world. During this era, there was a dramatic return to seeking supernatural explanations for mental illness.

"Treatment" of the mentally ill became focused on the exorcism of evil spirits, and many unfortunates were labeled as witches and were flogged, mutilated, starved, or burned alive. The idea that the mentally ill were possessed by demons persisted in some regions into the nineteenth century.

During this era, Middle Eastern countries were more enlightened than their European counterparts in all areas of medicine and psychology. Although spiritual theories had some followers in the Muslim world, many physicians looked more to the Greeks' conceptualization of mental illness. Some of these physicians furthered the understanding of mental disorders by categorizing and defining their clinical observations. Najab ud-din Unhammad (870–925), an Arab Islamic physician, identified nine categories of mental illness, including lovesickness with anxiety and depression, and anxious and ruminative states of doubt (obsessions and compulsions). The Persian physician Avicenna (980–1037) was one of the greatest scholars of early Islamic science. Avicenna and another Islamic physician of this era, Ishaq ibn Amram, both described melancholy (depression) in a manner that is very familiar to us today. Not only did Avicenna describe the melancholic person as irritable (a symptom shared with anxiety), but he also identified exaggerated fearfulness as a common personality trait. Ishaq ibn Amram acknowledged agitation, worry, and anxiety as symptoms of melancholy.

### An Emerging Light

Fortunately, as the Middle Ages progressed, there were gradual gains in philosophy and scholarship throughout Europe. Contact with the Islamic world also increased the access to Greek and Muslim scholarship. As a result, philosophers and the proliferation of medieval universities were again setting the tone for science, medicine, and psychology. During this period, a very significant contribution was made by the scholar Albertus Magnus (1193–1280). Against the wishes of the Church, Magnus reviewed all of Aristotle's writings and made them once again accessible to scientists. Roger Bacon (1214–1292) and Thomas Aquinas (1225–1274) followed in Magnus's footsteps and promoted the work of Greek and Roman authors. Aquinas attempted, as St. Augustine had done before him, to reconcile Christian thought and the rationalism of the Greek philosophers. The movement towards the Renaissance had begun.

## THE FOURTEENTH THROUGH SEVENTEENTH CENTURIES

The European Renaissance, lasting from approximately the fourteenth to the seventeenth centuries, is considered to be the bridge between the Middle Ages and the modern era. Building on the work of the thirteenth-century philosophers, there was a significant shift in the fifteenth century toward scientific thinking and rationalism. Although the growth occurred sporadically and conflicted with the teachings of the Catholic Church, this was the real beginning of the return to intellectual thought and scientific inquiry. Born in France, René Descartes (1596–1650) is often considered the father of modern Western philosophy. Descartes's contribution to psychology lies in his ideas about the mind and the role of thinking and rationality. Descartes, a deductive-rationalist philosopher, once said, "Cogito ergo sum," which is translated as "I think, therefore I am."

Descartes also accepted the concept of mind-body dualism, which enters into psychological and medical discussions to this day. He viewed the body as a machine that operated under the laws of physics. The mind, however, was an ethereal entity, lacking in substance, which operated by its own principles. Descartes proposed that the mind and body are joined and "compose a certain unity." This theory was the first to propose a true bidirectionality between the mind and the body, where the mind and body mutually influence each other. Heretofore, the thinking had essentially been that the body influenced the mind, but the mind did not influence the body. This is a key concept in the study of anxiety disorders.

Meanwhile, the Chinese further developed their thinking and treatment of mental disorders. They believed that emotional stability was achieved by an optimistic attitude and moderation in behavior and thought. Since the

Chinese believed that harmony was the natural order of life, they emphasized balance in all areas of social, political, medical, and artistic existence. During the Ming dynasty, acupuncture was used successfully to treat mental disorders on the basis of the theory that dysfunctions were caused by an imbalance in yin and yang and Confucius's five elements of wood, fire, metal, earth, and water. Chinese philosophers also identified the five basic human emotions as sorrow, fear, anger, desire, and joy.

In fifteenth-century Europe, scholars began to consider psychological processes and human emotions as more biological than spiritual in nature. Psychiatry began to return to the realm of physicians and scientists. In 1621, Robert Burton (1576–1640), who suffered from severe depression himself, published a book titled *Anatomy of Melancholy*. He was the first scholar to separate "madness" from melancholy and anxiety. Burton concluded that life circumstances and events, such as obsessive worrying and preoccupation with fears, could lead to melancholy, a notion that has been borne out empirically in the twentieth century. He also described what we know today as the anxiety disorder obsessive-compulsive disorder. Burton wrote of one individual

> who dared not to go over a bridge, come near a pool, rock, steep hill, lie in a chamber where cross-beams were, for fear he'd be tempted to hang, drown, or precipitate himself. In a silent auditorium, as at a sermon, he was afraid he shall speak aloud at unawares, something indecent, unfit to be said. (Burton, 1621, p. 253)

Burton recommended that people share their sadness or worry with sympathetic listeners and distract themselves from these negative emotions. Unfortunately, because he was not part of the medical profession, little attention was given to his book or his suggestions. Burton did, however, make recommendations that later became accepted practices in psychotherapy.

Thomas Willis (1621–1675), an Oxford-educated physician, was the founder of what came to be known as biological psychiatry. He proposed that mental disorders were related to nerve transmission, not blood circulation (humors). In 1664, Willis published *Cerebri Anatome*, a book detailing the history of the study of the brain. He studied brain anatomy and explained the behavioral consequences of brain function. Willis coined the term *neurology* to describe the study of the brain and nervous system and used the word *psychology* to describe the workings of the "mind." Willis recommended soothing and pleasurable activities for depressed and anxious individuals, yet he still supported beatings, restraint, bloodletting, and laxatives for the treatment of the "mad."

## The Interesting Story of Hysteria

Identified by Hippocrates and Plato, hysteria is a condition that was attached to female patients well into the twentieth century. The root of the word hysteria is *hystera*, which is Greek for uterus. The ancient theory was that the uterus took to wandering throughout the body, moving into the chest area and strangling the woman. This brought about fainting, nervousness, insomnia, abdominal heaviness, irritability, shortness of breath, loss of appetite for food or sex, and a "tendency to cause trouble."

Thomas Willis was the first to propose that hysteria was a nervous disorder. By carefully observing hysterical patients, Thomas Sydenham distinguished the phenomena of what we today call the somatoform disorders, which are disorders in which symptoms of medical disorder(s) (e.g., blindness, pain, paralysis, and convulsions) are present that cannot be accounted for by an actual medical condition.

In the nineteenth century, Paul Briquet (1796–1881) distinguished what we now call somatization disorder (also known as Briquet's syndrome), which presents with a wide range of gastrointestinal and reproductive system complaints along with a variety of sites of pain or discomfort (not considered an anxiety disorder). His observations also led him to dispel the notions that sexual frustration was the root cause of hysteria and that it was a strictly female malady. Briquet also proposed that the combination of predisposition (vulnerability) and life experiences (especially parental mistreatment) led to the development of hysteria.

Ernst von Feuchtersleben (1806–1849), an Austrian psychiatrist, identified the collection of hysteric symptoms we now know as histrionic personality disorder. This personality disorder is defined by an ongoing pattern of excessive emotionality and attention seeking. Although biological influences play a role in the etiology of personality disorders, they tend to be thought of as more the result of environmental influences. Despite the work of Sydenham and Willis, physicians in the nineteenth century still used the broader diagnostic view of hysteria and focused much of their practice on women who were so-called hysterics. Sigmund Freud largely built his theories and practice of psychoanalysis on the study of this group of patients.

Hysteria no longer exists as a diagnostic category. Collections of symptoms that fell into this catch-all syndrome have been reclassified into other psychiatric classifications, including personality disorders. In addition to histrionic personality disorder and the less frequently seen somatoform and dissociative disorders, many of the symptoms fall into the category of the anxiety disorders.

Thomas Sydenham (1624–1689) strongly valued empirical observation. His work regarding hysteria provided a significant contribution to the evolving study of mental health. Sydenham looked to temperament, emotion, psychological defenses, social pressures, and an individual's family situation to explain the development of many mental disorders. He also proposed that some mental disorders were organic in nature and resulted from actual physical disease processes. This etiological viewpoint, or emphasis on the origins of disease, was revolutionary. Sydenham's approach was much more holistic and systemic than had ever been considered previously.

## THE EIGHTEENTH CENTURY

George Cheyne (1671–1743) was a British society physician who wrote a book in 1733 titled *The English Malady*, which described an illness that directly affects the "nerves." He studied those suffering from anxiety and hypochondria, and he concluded that these were physical disorders over which the mind has no control. Cheyne's popular theory proved to be a catalyst for the growing practices of "nerve doctors."

Scottish scientist William Cullen (1710–1790) viewed mental illness as biologically based and influenced by an individual's environment and life experiences. He coined the term *neuroses* to categorize what he viewed as neurologically based mental illnesses or those occurring, he theorized, because of inflamed or irritated nerves. Cullen and Robert Whytt (1714–1766), who also did research in this area, interpreted neuroses as being caused by a disturbance in the flow of the nervous system, essentially "vapors." This view persisted for more than a century.

Some anxiety disorders and mild to moderate melancholia had, up to this point, been relatively neglected. Anxiety disorders generally fell into the catch-all realm of hysteria. People who suffered from melancholy and what we now call generalized anxiety disorder either endured their tribulations or spent time at a spa. Obsessive-compulsive disorder, however, fell into the category of psychosis, as did severe depression. These people were usually treated in asylums.

## THE NINETEENTH CENTURY

### Evolution: A Different Take on Human Behavior

In 1872, Charles Darwin (1809–1882), the English anthropologist and naturalist, published *The Expression of Emotion in Man and Animals*. He

**Figure 2.2** Historians have hypothesized that Charles Darwin may have suffered from panic disorder. (Photographer: Julia Margaret Cameron. Courtesy of Library of Congress, Prints and Photographs Division, LC-USZ62-52389)

recognized that this ability to express emotions began at birth and therefore was likely innate. He theorized that the expression of emotions evolved in many species as a survival mechanism. Darwin's focus on facial expression and posture began the tradition of studying emotion in both human and animal psychology. Scientists have since broadened their exploration of the physiological indicators of emotion. Examples of this include blood flow, respiration, and electrical activity in the brain. Darwin particularly focused on the expression of fear, from the activation of increased scanning of the environment to full-blown terror. His work emphasized that both humans and animals utilize facial expression as a component in the physiological response of fight or flight. This reaction, therefore, contributes to the survival of a species.

## Charles Darwin's Anxiety

Historians now believe that Charles Darwin suffered from panic disorder. His health problems began after his famous five-year voyage as a naturalist aboard the *Beagle*. Thomas Barloon and Russell Noyes, Jr., scientists from the University of Iowa, recently scrutinized Darwin's autobiography and other writings. Based on today's *DSM-IV-TR*, they concluded that Darwin met nine of the thirteen criteria for panic disorder. Questions remain about the validity of this theory, since Darwin suffered from a variety of other symptoms, and the panic symptoms individually could be explained by other illnesses.

Darwin's adult life was wracked with bouts of nausea, chest pain, palpitations, dizziness, abdominal distress, and terrifying nightmares. He retreated to the country and traveled only in the company of his family and house staff. Darwin reorganized his notebooks from his expeditions on the *Beagle* repeatedly and did not publish them for many years for fear of a negative response from the public and other scholars. He was exceedingly sensitive to public disparagement and ridicule. In an attempt to relieve his anxiety symptoms, Darwin often visited the English spa at Malvern. Barloon and Noyes theorize that Darwin's misery severely limited his activities and may have allowed the solitude and time to develop his theories on evolutionary progression and natural selection. Darwin wrote that "ill health, though it has annihilated several years of my life, has saved me from the distraction of society and its amusements" (Darwin, 1887, p.85).

## Continued Evolution of the Classification of Mental Disorders

Scientists have continually struggled to organize mental phenomena into a universal reference. Emil Kraepelin (1856–1926) was a German physician who is recognized for his extensive attempts to classify the mental disorders and to make sense of observable mental phenomena. The *DSM* series is based on Kraepelin's work. Confining his research to individuals within the mental asylums of his day, Kraepelin collected detailed case studies and recorded longitudinal studies over the lifetimes of his patients. This empirical evidence resulted in the classification of syndromes and subclassifications based on symptoms and courses of illness; it therefore improved differentiation between disorders. Kraepelin believed that many mental illnesses were biologically based. He identified affective (emotional) disorders, including the milder forms of mental disorders, such as neuroses, hysteria, and fright (panic disorder). Kraepelin believed that these disorders were psychogenic in origin rather than biologically based.

# 3

# The Development of Modern
# Approaches to Anxiety Disorders

## EARLY DEVELOPMENT OF SPECIFIC TREATMENTS FOR
## ANXIETY AND "HYSTERIA"

Dating back to ancient Greece, there has been a history of providing retreats where those who suffered from physical and mental illness could go to recover. In addition, the severely mentally ill needed to be protected from society, and in some cases, society needed to be protected from them. Unfortunately, these facilities varied over the centuries as to how humane and helpful they actually were.

By the nineteenth century, the public, especially the middle class, became reluctant to send their family members to such institutions. Psychiatrists, the majority of whom worked in asylums and were called alienists at the time, were not viewed as helpers but rather as enemies. A diagnosis of mental illness was seen as a condemnation of the family. This prompted the field of psychiatry to redefine mental illness as "nerve problems." Defining all mental problems, including psychosis, as nervous became the new trend, since nervous problems were attributed to life's difficulties or to an organic irritation of the nerves.

Fortunately, many neurologists and general medical practitioners focused on treating the "truly nervous," that is, those with anxiety or mild psychiatric disorders. Some practitioners began to specialize in this area at the health resorts and mineral baths of Europe. These early private practices and spas of Europe mostly treated affluent women who led comfortable, but meaningless lives, and who were suffering from the "vapors." The spa movement gradually encompassed those with hysteria, hypochondria, exhaustion, and anxiety disorders.

Meanwhile, in the United States, George Beard (1839–1883), a New York physician, coined the term *neurasthenia* to describe a physiological malady centered in the nerves. This vague catch-all diagnosis resembled hysteria and was characterized by fatigue, aches and pains, weakness, loss of appetite and weight, and diminished memory. (A subclassification of this diagnosis is defined today as chronic fatigue syndrome.) In the nineteenth and early twentieth centuries, neurasthenia was known as "tired nerves" and was a very popular diagnosis in both America and Europe. The "rest cure" was developed by Silas Weir Mitchell (1829–1914), who found that patients with neurasthenia responded well to bed rest, isolation, a milk diet with forced feeding, electrical treatment, and massage.

The Weir Mitchell cure caught on like wildfire in Europe. Spas embraced this method of treatment, and private clinics and lodgings, called hysterical homes, were established and once again supported the notion that it was the nerves that caused mental distress. By 1900, the Weir Mitchell cure was the treatment of choice for a wide range of neurotic complaints. Neurologists, who were the primary clinicians (psychiatrists being still largely in the asylums treating the "insane"), began to notice that the cure depended on the nature of the one-to-one relationship between the physician and patient. They discovered that this relationship provided the active ingredient in the Weir Mitchell cure, which also led to the conclusion that neurasthenia was much more psychological than physiological. Neurologists began to further explore the aspects of the therapeutic relationship and realized that taking an interest in their patients and giving specific advice were the key elements in the therapy. Modern psychotherapy was born.

Neurologists and alienists in private practice also attempted to expand the methods of treatment for their "nervous" patients. The theory and practice of psychoanalysis developed in this environment of community-based private practitioners. This trend toward private practice and the development of psychoanalysis also helped psychiatrists move out of the asylum setting and established them as therapists. They eventually surpassed neurologists in that role. Psychoanalysis further built on the strength and effectiveness of the doctor-patient relationship and became the primary treatment method for neuroses.

## MAJOR INFLUENCES IN THE DEVELOPMENT OF PSYCHOANALYSIS

Because of their work with hypnotism in relieving some patients of their nervous symptoms, physicians Franz Anton Mesmer (1734–1815) and James

Braid (1795–1860) strongly promoted the concept of the unconscious, which provided the basis for psychoanalytic theory.

Jean-Martin Charcot (1825–1893), another significant contributor to psychoanalytic thinking, is considered to be the father of clinical neurology. His work resulted in the identification of multiple sclerosis and amyotrophic lateral sclerosis (Lou Gehrig's disease) and furthered the research on Parkinson's disease. These discoveries and other progress in clinical neurology provided the ability to finally distinguish patients who had true neurological disorders from patients who were merely nervous. Many people previously diagnosed as suffering from hypochondria or hysteria were now correctly diagnosed with the aforementioned disorders or genuine paralysis and were considered to be physically ill. Charcot's research on hysteria led to the discovery that hypnosis could alter, eliminate, or induce hysterical symptoms.

Austrian neurologist Sigmund Freud (1856–1939) was a junior colleague of Josef Breuer (1842–1925), a Viennese physician. Breuer is famous for his controversial work with a young woman, referred to as Anna O, who suffered from a classic case of hysteria. Through the use of hypnosis, Breuer helped her express, sometimes quite intensely, her repressed, or consciously forgotten, emotions about her life experiences. Freud collaborated with Breuer in developing a method that prompted hysterical patients to express emotionally traumatic events that were too distressing to be faced on a conscious level. The scientists concluded that the cure for hysteria was to unblock repressed feelings. Breuer found this work to be too intense and took issue with Freud's emphasis on sexual memories; he eventually pulled out of the collaboration.

Many of Freud's contemporaries strongly disagreed with his emphasis on childhood sexuality, and his dogmatic approach alienated many scholars, although he undoubtedly deserves credit for organizing the thinking of his predecessors into a coherent theory. However, since the unconscious is not observable, Freud's theory was based more on speculation than empirical science. Freud also rejected the notion of classification systems for mental illness and instead focused on the experiences, fantasies, dreams, conflicts, and emotions of the individual.

### Freud's Psychoanalytic Theory in a Nutshell (or the Role of Anxiety in Psychoanalytic Theory)

Building on the work of Mesmer, Charcot, Breuer, and others, Sigmund Freud embraced the idea of the unconscious and the curative effect of the expression of repressed thoughts and feelings. He developed the idea that instinctual sexual drives, as well as child rearing techniques, play a significant

## Freud's Own Anxiety

Historians believe that much of Freud's thinking about psychological phenomena was the result of his own self-analysis. Biographers refer to his self-doubt and insecurity regarding his ability and intelligence and his need for reassurance, approval, and emotional support. Freud suffered all his life from anxiety concerning his personal finances and was fearful of "modern contrivances." He was so anxious about leaving his native Vienna that he did so only when the Nazi occupation made it unsafe for him to remain there. He also experienced psychosomatic symptoms and depression. Although he suffered from depression and anxiety, his self-analysis resulted in a very productive period for him in the development of his theories and treatment methodology. Had he not been plagued by his own inner struggles, Freud might have never developed such an influential system of thought and treatment.

**Figure 3.1** Freud's thinking about psychological phenomena may have stemmed in part from his own self-analysis. (Courtesy of National Library of Medicine)

role in the psychosexual development of a child. Freud believed that certain drives had to be dealt with at different developmental periods. He posited that if these drives are frustrated or conflicted they will cause the individual to develop significant anxiety problems (neuroses).

According to Freud's theory, there are three parts of the personality: the id, ego, and superego. The id represents the biological impulses, and the ego is the mediating entity that operates to get needs met and also to reconcile the demands of the superego. The superego is the moral compass of the personality. The id, ego, and superego are believed to be in constant conflict; consequently, the very essence of life is to manage anxiety. If managed ineffectively, the results will be the manifestation of defense mechanisms and mental disorders. If the resulting anxiety is extremely intense, the individual may become fixated in the developmental stage where the conflict occurs. This results in a personality disorder.

Freud proposed that symptoms reflected the psychological experiences and that the expression of the underlying feelings, fantasies, memories, and conflicts would bring about a cure. He viewed the psychological process of burying undesirable memories, impulses, and conflicts as something engaged in by all humans and defined the resulting perspectives and behaviors as defense mechanisms against anxiety, threat, and psychic pain. He saw the defense mechanisms as adaptive strategies, albeit often self-defeating ones. A key defense mechanism that Freud identified is repression, in which traumatic memories are buried in the unconscious. This process requires considerable energy, and it generates much anxiety and ultimately leads to neuroses. Essentially, Freud built his theories around the adaptation of the individual to anxieties inherent in human development and early experiences. Examples of manifestations of internal conflicts include obsessions and compulsions, general nervousness, panic attacks, and hypochondriasis.

As the twentieth century progressed, Emil Kraepelin's biologically based theories were eschewed in favor of the psychoanalytic view, which proposed and built its therapeutic approach on the idea that all mental illness was due primarily to environmental factors, child rearing, and life events. Although psychoanalytic theory lacked any empirical validity, its original popularity in the Victorian era and growing popular acceptance encouraged psychiatrists to embrace its tenets, and the psychoanalytic movement spread throughout Europe and America.

## THE DEVELOPMENT OF BEHAVIORAL PSYCHOLOGY

The roots of behavioral psychology are found in the classical Greek writings, particularly those left to us by Aristotle. Ivan Pavlov (1849–1936) and

Edward Thorndike (1874–1949), who laid out the principles of classical and operant conditioning, respectively, launched the study of learning in the modern era. Besides illustrating how a type of learning takes place, Pavlov and his fellow research physiologists also found that fear could be conditioned in a similar manner. This led ultimately to the greater understanding of the acquisition of fears and anxieties. In the 1920s, the principles of learning began to be applied to personality development, the acquisition of abnormal behaviors, and eventually mental disorders.

The founders and developers of behavioral psychology, or behaviorism, highly valued the application of the scientific method to academic psychology. The first program in experimental psychology was established by Wilhelm Wundt (1832–1920) in 1879 at the University of Leipzig. Because mental processes are unobservable and subjective, the behaviorists felt that these processes fell outside the realm of the scientific approach. Instead, they focused on observable behaviors and their acquisition and description.

John Watson (1878–1959) is considered to be the founder of behavioral psychology. He was a strict and absolute behaviorist, proposing that all human behavior, personality, and aberration could be explained by learning principles. He published an article in 1913 in *Psychology Review* titled "Psychology as the Behaviorist Views It." The article was both controversial and provocative because it rejected the use of introspection and the study of conscious (and certainly unconscious) processes as ways to understand human behavior and mental disorders.

Watson and his wife, Rosalie Rayner (1899–1935), were the first to produce a learned fear response in a human subject. Combining a loud noise, which they knew produced trembling and crying in eleven-month-old "Little Albert," with the presentation of the benign stimulus of a white rat, they were able to induce anxiety and fear reactions in the child to the white rat alone (classical conditioning). They also discovered that Little Albert's fear generalized to other white furry animals as well. Another associate of Watson's, Mary Cover Jones (1896–1987), used learning principles to extinguish (eliminate) a fear response in another child, Peter, who was afraid of white furry animals. After observing other children fearlessly play with a white rat, Peter began to show less fear of the animal. In another experiment, Jones had Peter encounter a white rabbit in graduated steps until he was able to handle the rabbit without fear. Jones was the first researcher to use behavioral strategies as a therapeutic tool, and she published her results in 1924.

Burrhus Frederic (B.F.) Skinner (1904–1990) embraced behaviorism during his education at Harvard and continued to build on the work of Pavlov, Thorndike, and Watson. Skinner's experiments with operant conditioning

**Figure 3.2** Mary Cover Jones was the first researcher to use behavioral strategies as a therapeutic tool. (Courtesy of G. Paul Bishop, Jr.)

(rats pushing a lever for the reward of food) and his contraptions for measuring response rates, later dubbed Skinner boxes, helped delineate some of the crucial principles in learning and behavioral psychology.

Although opinionated and contentious, Skinner effectively publicized behaviorism in academic circles and to the general public. Luckily the researchers, known as neo-behaviorists, who followed these early pioneers of behavioral psychology softened their approach and were less adamant about the absolutism of behaviorism in explaining all of behavior, including mental illness. This allowed for a gradual melding of behavioral theory with the research in clinical psychiatry.

In 1947, O.H. Mowrer (1907–1982) described a two-factor model utilizing both classical and operant conditioning to explain the acquisition and maintenance of fear and anxiety. He proposed that fear is acquired through classical conditioning and maintained by operant conditioning; avoiding the stimulus brings relief (reinforcement). Researchers later observed that avoidance responses to a fear-conditioned stimulus are very hardy and are difficult to extinguish.

### Movement away from Strict Behaviorism

Edward Chase Tolman (1886–1959) was the first true cognitive-behaviorist and introduced the concept and role of cognitions into behavioral theory. Tolman proposed that there are intervening variables of acquired knowledge, experience, and reasoning that influence stimulus-response learning. Internal thought processes give people choices and decision-making ability above and beyond simple operant conditioning. Behavior could consequently be goal-directed and purposive.

A major breakthrough in cognitive theory evolved from the work of Yale colleagues John Dollard (1900–1980) and Neal Miller (1909–2000). They conceptualized that fear and anxiety are acquired through conditioned learning and compared them to inner drives as identified in psychoanalytic theory. Miller later researched the acquisition and extinction of physiological responses (e.g., increased heart rate and respiration) and determined that they follow the same learning rules as voluntary responses. This theory helps to explain how the physiological response to anxiety-provoking stimuli becomes established and maintained. Their approach evolved into a cognitive learning approach combining the concepts of the conscious and the unconscious, as well as cultural influences, social learning, and behaviorism.

Working independently, Joseph Wolpe (1915–1997) and Hans Eysenck (1916–1997) both dismissed Dollard and Miller's incorporation of psychoanalytic theory into behavioral theory and rejected the notion of conflicting drives. Wolpe and Eysenck proposed that an innate, physiological vulnerability to anxiety explained the development of an anxiety disorder or other mental illness. They believed that when a patient who suffered from anxiety sensitivity later experienced intense anxiety that became associated with a perceived actual or not-actual threat, then that patient would develop a mental disorder, specifically anxiety or phobias.

Wolpe was a physician who served as a medical officer in the South African army during World War II. He treated many cases of "war neuroses"—what we now designate posttraumatic stress disorder (PTSD)—and realized that the drug therapy that was offered was unsuccessful. He understood the neurotic fear response that could be conditioned, and following the example of Jones, he developed a means of extinguishing that response. Wolpe began with a less fearful proximity to the object, such as a mental image or a picture, and escalated toward more difficult presentations until, eventually, the person was introduced to the actual, up-close stimulus. In addition, Wolpe coupled the exposure to the stimulus with an opposite physiological response achieved through relaxation training. He called this systematic desensitization. Wolpe emphasized the importance of actual (in vivo) exposure to the feared object and recommended that patients continue to do in vivo exposures at home between therapy sessions. Wolpe's research laid the foundation for the development of exposure-based treatment for anxiety disorders, especially phobias and obsessive-compulsive disorder.

In 1971, Arnold Lazarus (1932–), a psychologist and researcher who originated the term behavior therapy, published *Behavior Therapy and Beyond,* which criticized the strict adherence to behavioral strategies. He saw these strategies as too mechanistic and dogmatic and felt they limited the comprehensive assessment and understanding of the individual. Lazarus's text was the first significant publication to outline a form of cognitive-behavioral therapy (CBT) and accelerated the acceptance and support of more cognitively based approaches. Cognitive-behavioral theory and therapy began to blossom.

## THE DEVELOPMENT OF COGNITIVE-BEHAVIORAL APPROACHES

George Kelly (1905–1967) had a crucial influence on cognitive-behavioral theory through his development of personal construct theory, which he published in 1955. Kelly proposed that humans exist in two worlds: first, the world that exists outside of ourselves; and second, the world as we interpret it in our constructs or representations. A personal construct is the way in which an individual understands or construes the world. Constructs help predict what will happen and how to react appropriately. Constructs grow ever more complex over time, since we are able to validate or alter our constructs as we integrate new disconfirming or confirming information. If an individual continues to embrace faulty constructs, a mental disorder may result.

Psychologist Albert Ellis (1913–2007), although trained as a psychoanalyst, furthered the development of CBT. Because of a difficult early life and his own experience with severe social anxiety, Ellis became an interactive and directive therapist focused on problem solving. He discovered that his patients seemed to be driven by their erroneous interpretations of their experiences, which had an impact on both their emotions and their behavior. Ellis helped his patients identify their irrational and illogical beliefs and replace those beliefs with more rational thoughts and action. He also encouraged self-dialogue, whereby patients could learn to challenge their beliefs on their own. By 1955, Ellis had abandoned the practice of psychoanalysis in favor of what he termed rational emotive therapy, which is now called rational emotive behavior therapy (REBT). He continually emphasized the concept that problems can be solved, and he applied REBT to anxiety disorders and a variety of other disorders and problems.

Psychiatrist Aaron Timothy Beck (1921–) also had considerable anxieties of his own to face. Like Ellis, he later abandoned his psychoanalytic orientation. Beck discovered that depressed patients had a preponderance of cognitive errors that were negative and self-limiting. Although the depression itself may influence thinking in a negative direction, it is escalating negative automatic thoughts and schemata (frames of reference) that contribute to a downward spiral toward hopelessness. This cycle maintains and exacerbates the

**Figure 3.3** Dr. Aaron Beck has been instrumental in the development of cognitive-behavioral therapy. (Courtesy of Dr. Aaron T. Beck)

depression. With these findings, Beck went on to develop his theories and methods for cognitive therapy. He also incorporated behavioral components, such as exposure and systematic desensitization, into the cognitive treatment.

Other significant contributors to cognitive-behavioral therapy include Albert Bandura (1925–), Donald Meichenbaum, Judith Beck, David Burns, and S.J. Rachman. Rachman has also done considerable work in the areas of fear and courage and childhood anxiety.

## THE ROLE OF THEORIES OF EMOTION IN THE CONCEPTUALIZATION OF ANXIETY

Much of our understanding of anxiety and its disorders comes from the theorists and researchers who have studied anxiety as an emotion. Today, it is widely accepted that emotion is made up of the following three components: (1) expressive behaviors, such as facial expression and posture; (2) the functioning of biology and the nervous system; and (3) cognitive appraisal. Until the latter part of the twentieth century, research often focused on a singular element and gave little attention to the integration of the three components.

### Emotion as Expressive Behaviors

Charles Darwin set the stage for the understanding of emotions as innate survival and communication mechanisms. His work continues to be supported by empirical evidence that there is a consistent fear system that is innate, or hard-wired, in humans. Scientists have since built on his theory, introducing the cognitive component and, through neuroimaging, examining the brain mechanisms involved in the experience of and response to emotion.

Today, it is generally agreed that fear is a fundamental and basic emotion that is essential for survival. Fear is universal across species, cultures, and races. Anxiety, on the other hand, is seen as a more complicated, perhaps secondary emotion. Carroll Izard (1924–) proposed that anxiety is a blend of a variety of emotions, such as distress, anger, sadness, guilt, and shame, along with the predominant basic emotion of fear. He further states that an individual develops an anxious personality when "inflexible" affective-cognitive structures are established through learning and repetition.

### Neurobiological Theories

Walter Cannon (1871–1945) was a Harvard physiologist whose major work focused on the role of physiological changes associated with emotional experience. In 1915 he published *Bodily Changes in Pain, Hunger, Fear, and Rage*, and in 1923, he published *Traumatic Shock*, which presented his research with World War I soldiers on what we know as PTSD. Cannon viewed emotion as a function of the brain that was primarily due to activity in the hypothalamus, with some controlling function seated in the cerebral cortex. He also identified the chemical mediation of autonomic nerve impulses across the synapse (see Figures 5.3a and 5.3b).

Scientific research begun in the 1970s led to the discovery of genetic and physical abnormalities in the brain that pointed to multivector theories of causation in mental disorders. By the 1980s, there was a tremendous leap in the understanding of the inherited tendencies of anxiety disorders and the role of brain mechanisms and neurotransmitters. Further delineation of the subtypes of anxiety disorders occurred during this period of growth. Today, neurobiology is always considered to be a factor in anxiety and its disorders. Many theorists believe it is primary and causal in the development of anxiety disorders.

### Cognitive Appraisal

In 1962, Stanley Schachter (1922–1997) and Jerome Singer (1924–) published their results on the relationship of cognitive appraisal to emotion. Simply stated, their theory proposed that people experience physiological arousal when exposed to certain events. We then give meaning, or a cognitive interpretation, to the state we experience.

Conversely, Richard Lazarus (1922–2002) theorized that cognition is primary and that our appraisal of events determines the emotional response. Unfortunately, both theories are too simplistic and contradictory, and they ignore irrational or unexplained ("Why am I feeling this way?") emotional responses.

In the 1980s Robert Zajonc (1923–2008), who was more in the behavioral camp, proposed that humans can experience emotion, encode emotional information, and respond behaviorally without cognitive evaluation. He believed that affect comes first and is primary. There is evidence, however, that information can be processed via established schemata or cognitive sets outside of one's awareness, which could, therefore, precede emotion.

Peter Lang's bioinformational approach addresses some of the contradictions and questions discussed above. He emphasizes the processing of information, which can take into account the out-of-consciousness appraisal that can occur when one is confronted with an emotion-provoking event. Lang proposes that there are "data files" that hold learned plus innate response and meaning propositions, which allow for the rapid processing of information. For an emotional response to occur, a variety of these propositions need to come together. Lang views emotions as action tendencies. According to Lang, some responses are specific and focused, such as a phobia of spiders, whereas other response sets are diffuse, such as those experienced with generalized anxiety disorder. Lang's work has also led to the present-day emphasis on integrated models of emotion, which take into account all three components: behavioral, biological, and cognitive.

By the end of the twentieth century, cognitive attribution and appraisal theories were found to be very popular among clinicians, and research had shown the related therapy (CBT) to be effective in many cases. Today, theorists see emotion-cognition interactions not as a linear progression but rather as an enormously complex relationship with a variety of routes possible in terms of information processing, perception, cognitive appraisal, and memory.

## THE HISTORY OF PSYCHOPHARMACOLOGICAL INTERVENTIONS WITH ANXIETY

### Early Chemical Efforts to Deal with Anxiety

Since prehistoric times, humans have employed mood-altering substances to cope with stress and fear. One of the earliest substances used for this purpose was ethanol (that is, alcohol), which is made by fermenting fruits, vegetables, or grain. Alcohol is a central nervous system depressant and therefore causes sedation and relaxation. Alcohol may still be the primary substance used to self-manage anxiety and stress.

Archeological evidence has revealed that opium was discovered in Europe as early as 4000 BCE. Extracted from a particular poppy plant, *Papaver somniferum*, opium has been called the joy plant. It is considered a sedative-hypnotic and has properties that depress the central nervous system and induce relaxation and sleep. Hippocrates, Galen, Thomas Sydenham, Robert Burton, and many other scientists have acknowledged opium's usefulness in medicine. Sydenham is alleged to have stated, "Among the remedies which it has pleased Almighty God to give to man to relieve his sufferings, none is so universal and so efficacious as opium." In 1527, Swiss alchemist and physician Paracelsus (Phillip von Hohenheim) (1493–1541) introduced opium into the European medical literature in the form of laudanum (literally, "something to be praised"), which is a mixture of alcohol and an opium derivative. In 1680, Sydenham concocted his own blend of laudanum, which consisted of opium and sherry plus herbs and spices. Cinnamon was a particularly favorite ingredient because it added a pleasant taste to the concoction.

Opium has been used since the 1500s to relieve pain, induce sleep, diminish stress, and remedy unpleasant emotions and nervousness. Laudanum was once a staple in the medicine cabinets of most homes and was even given to infants and children regularly for distress, colic, and a variety of illnesses. The use of opium in Europe exploded in the nineteenth century. Readily available in pharmacies, opium was used by all social classes to deal with the boredom and stresses of life.

---

### A Disastrous Pharmaceutical Development

A German chemist, Heinrich Dreser (1860–1924), led the Bayer Company of Germany to refine and launch two of the world's most famous drugs, one of which was aspirin. In 1874, Dreser diluted the active ingredient of opium (morphine) with acetyls and created diacetylmorphine. This new substance was given the brand name Heroin. Commercially released by the Bayer Company in 1898, Heroin was originally thought to be less addictive than morphine and was marketed as a pain reliever and cough suppressant. Unfortunately, Heroin turned out to be even more potent and, consequently, even more addictive than morphine. Clinical reports, deaths, and cases of serious addiction prompted Bayer to pull Heroin from the market in 1913, which proved to be an embarrassment for the company and damaged its reputation. Although Dreser experienced significant financial success for his development of aspirin, it is alleged that he himself became addicted to heroin later in life.

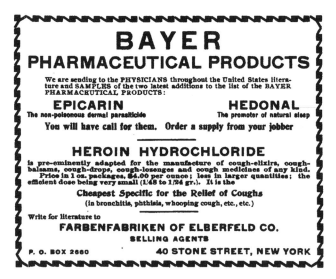

**Figure 3.4** This advertisement by Bayer appeared in the *American Journal of Pharmacology* in 1900. Heroin was marketed as a cheap and effective remedy for coughs.

## Other Nineteenth-Century Developments in Psychopharmacology

Bromide salts and chloral hydrate were used in the 1800s to alleviate anxiety and emotional distress. Discovered in 1826 in a salt marsh in England, bromide salts are also found in seawater. Potassium bromide, in particular, was discovered to have sedative and anticonvulsive properties. Used to induce sleep, it was also utilized for relieving seizures. Bromide salts are used today only as a veterinary anticonvulsant. Chloral hydrate, also a sedative, was first synthesized in 1832 and was heralded as a sleep remedy. In addition, it was used to help relieve anxiety and provide sedation for medical and dental procedures. Chloral hydrate has significant abuse potential since it is fast-acting and very addictive. Mixed with alcohol in Victorian England, it became a popular drink called a Mickey Finn.

Chloral hydrate and bromide salts were eventually replaced by barbiturates at the beginning of the twentieth century and later by benzodiazepines to help manage anxiety and stress. Chloral hydrate is still available in syrup form under the brand name Noctec, which is also approved for use in children. Often prescribed as a sleep aid, it is used for preoperative sedation and anxiety management, as well as postoperative pain management when combined with opiates and other pain medications. Chloral hydrate continues to pose problems in usage today.

Barbiturates were developed in the latter part of the nineteenth century. In 1864, German chemist and Nobel Prize winner Adolf von Baeyer (1835–1917) developed barbituric acid, the key component of barbiturate compounds. Barbiturates are central nervous system depressants and sedative-hypnotics that induce a relaxed state; they were used for the treatment of anxiety and insomnia in the first half of the twentieth century. They replaced opiates, bromide salts, and chloral hydrate for these purposes. In addition, barbiturates have anticonvulsant properties and are still prescribed for the treatment of seizure disorders. Barbiturates are also used in anesthesiology and in veterinary medicine to euthanize animals. Like the sedative-hypnotics that preceded them, barbiturates are also dangerous, highly addictive drugs that must be dosed very carefully since overdoses can occur easily and result in coma or death. Phenobarbital and Seconal are two common barbiturates in use today.

## The Search for Chemical Answers to Severe Mental Illness

Effective chemical treatments for severe mental disorders were not developed until the 1900s. The influenza epidemic of 1918 revitalized the interest in biological psychiatry because of the preponderance of residual psychotic symptoms resulting from the illness. Using the antihistamine chlorpromazine,

Parisian surgeon Henri Laborit (1914–1995) discovered a tremendous drop in presurgical anxiety for his patients and was able to use less anesthesia. Upon Laborit's suggestion, psychiatrist Pierre Deniker (1917–1998) used the drug with agitated and uncontrollable patients and had remarkable results. Chlorpromazine calmed many patients and allowed them to converse and resume a more normal life.

The pharmaceutical company Smith Kline bought the rights to chlorpromazine in 1952. The drug, under the brand name Thorazine, was introduced into the United States in 1954 and created a revolution in mental health care. Up to this point, the management of psychotic illnesses, such as schizophrenia, fell to the asylum system and was largely physical in nature. Patients had been restrained and secluded since there was no other way to control their symptoms.

Because of the enormous improvement in the management of the severely mentally ill that Thorazine initiated, medication research and drug development continued to focus on the amelioration of psychotic symptoms. New drugs helped reduce psychosis, and small doses of these antipsychotic medications, which are considered to be major tranquilizers, were used to treat anxiety.

In the 1950s, the neurotransmitters serotonin and dopamine were identified in the brain. Neurotransmitters are necessary for the transmission of electrical impulses from one nerve cell (neuron) to another. Early research on neurotransmitters focused on schizophrenia and other psychotic disorders, but it soon became apparent that the neurotransmitters were also implicated in depression.

Meanwhile, prior to the 1950s, amphetamines, which are known as "uppers" and "speed," were used to treat the low-energy and low-motivation symptoms of depression. Amphetamines were not as useful as anticipated and were also very addictive. Consequently, more efforts were channeled into research on finding effective antidepressant medications. In the 1950s, a chemical related to a drug used during World War II as an antibiotic in the treatment of tuberculosis was found to elevate low mood. This drug, iproniazid (Marsilid), has an effect on monoamines, chemicals that affect the neurotransmitters in the brain. Deficiencies in the neurotransmitters norepinephrine, serotonin, and dopamine were observed concurrently with depression. Iproniazid and related drugs were found to boost the levels of these neurotransmitters and to reduce depressive symptoms in some people. This development of the monoamine oxidase inhibitors (MAOIs) brought relief to many people suffering from depression. Unfortunately, MAOIs require certain dietary restrictions and have some unpleasant side effects.

In 1960, clinical trials in England with a drug called imipramine (Tofranil) were conducted. Although designed to combat psychotic symptoms, imipramine was found to change serotonin levels and to improve mood in depressed patients. Imipramine and its relatives were named tricyclics because of their molecular structure. This new class of antidepressants had fewer side effects and lacked the restrictions of the MAOIs.

Research with the tricyclic drugs also led to greater understanding of the reuptake mechanism in neurons. The tricyclics prevented the neurons from reabsorbing serotonin after it had been released into the synapse. More serotonin was consequently available in the synapse, which then reduced depression. Other examples of the class of tricyclics are clomipramine (Anafranil) and amitryptiline (Elavil).

As research trials and the regular use of antidepressants progressed, scientists discovered that MAOIs and the tricyclics also had antianxiety (anxiolytic) effects. This eventually led to the understanding that some of the same neurotransmitters that are involved in depression are also involved in anxiety. As a result of the discovery that antidepressants are effective with anxiety, psychiatrists began to use these drugs to treat anxiety symptoms.

### The Antianxiety Path

Frank Berger (1913–2008) had developed a muscle relaxant called mephenesin in the hopes of helping patients with Parkinson's disease. Although it failed to be useful for its intended purpose, Berger realized that the drug relieved anxiety for short periods of time. Later, Carter Products (known for Carter's Little Liver Pills) asked Berger to produce a mephenesin-like drug to relieve anxiety. Together with chemist Bernie Ludwig, he developed meprobamate, which functioned as a tranquilizer. Carter abandoned the project because the company surveyed physicians who reported that they had no need for an anxiety-reducing drug. A subsidiary of Carter eventually picked up the project.

The first drug specifically created to relieve anxiety, meprobamate (Miltown), was produced in 1950 and revolutionized the public's relationship with psychotherapeutics. Presented in 1955 at the annual meeting of the American Psychiatric Association, meprobamate caught on like wildfire. The demand for Miltown quickly outweighed the supply. Statistics report that in one particular month in 1956, one out of twenty Americans was taking a tranquilizer. Because of its sedating and addictive properties, meprobamate triggered a race to develop better anxiolytics.

Meanwhile, in the New Jersey lab of Hoffman-LaRoche (Roche), Leo Sternbach (1908–2005) discovered chlordiazepoxide, which had a relaxing effect on a colony of particularly rambunctious monkeys without reducing their alertness. In 1960, Roche marketed this drug, the first of the benzodiaze-pines, as Librium. Further research led to its sister drug, diazepam (Valium). One report in 1970 noted that one in five women and one in thirteen men were using tranquilizers.

Unfortunately, like meprobamate, the benzodiazepines turned out to be highly addictive. Each new benzodiazepine promised to be less addictive and have fewer side effects than its predecessor, but drugs in this class all have addictive properties. In 1975, the United States Food and Drug Administra-tion (FDA) instituted controls on the prescription of meprobamate and the benzodiazepines. The FDA's ruling and the dissemination of information about the hazards of these drugs significantly reduced their use. Despite benzodiaze-pines' tainted history, they are still used for short-term relief, for example, from the intense anxiety of panic attacks while waiting for longer acting medi-cation to take effect.

### The Antidepressant Link

The fact that antidepressants are effective with anxiety disorders gave physicians and patients an important alternative to the addictive benzodiaze-pines. Unfortunately, the tricyclic antidepressants also have numerous side effects that make them difficult for many patients to tolerate. The search for better drugs continued. Eli Lilly and Company developed a drug called fluoxe-tine in the 1970s that is a selective serotonin reuptake inhibitor (SSRI). It reduced the absorption of serotonin within the presynaptic cell and made more serotonin available. In the late 1970s, fluoxetine went into clinical trials, and the results were astonishing. Not only did it reduce depression, but it sig-nificantly diminished the undesirable side effects of the tricyclics, such as weight gain and constipation. In addition, fluoxetine had a safer therapeutic window, which is the margin between the therapeutic dosage range and a toxic dose. In 1987, the FDA approved fluoxetine (brand name Prozac), which was also found to be effective in treating anxiety and panic.

Prozac became society's new miracle drug. In addition to treating anxiety and depressive disorders, Prozac helped patients cope with life's stresses and strains even in the absence of an actual psychiatric disorder. Its popularity rose even more quickly than that of Valium. Books and articles have been published vilifying Prozac, and concerns were raised about its alleged potential for increas-ing suicidality, which is still being debated. Nevertheless, Prozac and its cousins, the newer SSRIs, continue to be highly regarded and utilized. New SSRI-type medications are still being developed, including sertraline (Zoloft), paroxetine (Paxil), fluvoxamine (Luvox), citalopram (Celexa), and escitalopram (Lexapro).

Like their predecessors, the SSRIs provide solutions but also pose problems. They can be agitating to certain patients and sometimes lose their effectiveness, so that increasingly higher dosages or a change in medication is necessary. Paxil has been found to have a withdrawal syndrome that is very unpleasant. Despite the problems, the SSRIs are the front-line medications for the treatment of most anxiety disorders. Other drugs, including the benzodiazepines and serotonin-norepinephrine reuptake inhibitors, such as Effexor, sometimes augment or replace the SSRIs.

## CONTINUED ADVANCES

In 1988, psychologist David Barlow published the seminal text *Anxiety and Its Disorders: The Nature and Treatment of Anxiety and Panic,* which analyzed previous research and presented his own findings. It was updated in 2002. With psychologist Edward Blanchard, Barlow founded the Center for Stress and Anxiety Disorders at the State University of New York at Albany as a teaching, research, and treatment facility. He and his colleagues, including Michelle Craske, Ron Rapee, and Richard Heimberg, have been particularly prolific in their research on anxiety disorders, especially panic disorder, generalized anxiety disorders, social phobia, and specific phobias. Along with psychologists Timothy Brown and Peter DiNardo, Barlow has developed the widely used and reliable assessment instrument, the *Anxiety Disorders Interview Schedule,* now in its fourth version.

Technological advances have also led us to new discoveries, which will be discussed in Chapter 5. Brain imaging, genetic research, and the study of neurochemistry and anatomy have shed much light on the etiology and mechanisms of anxiety. It is interesting to note that much of this evolution has come full circle to the research and theorizing of the ancient Greeks. Although they lacked the tools to explore anxiety and mental disorders to the extent that we have been able to, the Greeks' broad conceptualization of biological, psychological, and behavioral aspects of disorders was correct. Our understanding of anxiety certainly accelerated in the twentieth century and has led us to more comprehensive assessment and options for relatively effective treatment.

# 4

## The What, Who, and How of Anxiety Disorders

### THE ANXIETY DISORDERS

In the twenty-first century, we accept anxiety as a necessary emotion that is crucial for survival. The basic emotion of fear is hard-wired in our brains and, as a pure emotion, helps us respond to danger. Anxiety appears to be fear mixed with other emotions and is more diffuse than fear, but nevertheless, it helps us react to threats and plan appropriate strategies to resolve the situation.

Unfortunately, when the experience of anxiety interferes with daily activities and becomes a mental health disorder, it can be debilitating. Some people are genetically predisposed to be particularly sensitive to anxiety and can develop anxiety disorders when a critical combination of negative life events, environment, and learning (psychological vulnerabilities) occurs. When anxiety is more intense than necessary, attaches itself to objects or situations that are not truly dangerous, or is ever-present, it becomes problematic. Uncontrolled anxiety interferes with life and functioning and renders the person experiencing it miserable. Anxiety may cause problems with thinking, sleeping, eating, and functioning. It can be debilitating, hindering people's family, social, educational, and occupational circumstances. Anxiety disorders affect physical health, morbidity, health care costs, and workplace productivity.

**An Interrupted Life**

Chad, who presented for treatment at the age of twenty-four, had been considered a shy child. He had had trouble separating from his mother and was
leery of new situations. Chad also tended to worry about many insignificant
things that would preoccupy his thoughts at times. He eventually adjusted
well to school, but he tended to hang back and would interact with other
children only when invited. His parents encouraged him to participate in
hockey, for which he had a natural ability. This enabled Chad to make
friends with other boys on his team. Once he relaxed, his social skills were
actually quite good.

Chad completed high school and college with minor impairment from his
social anxiety. He disliked making presentations before his classmates, avoiding it
when possible, and was anxious meeting new people and attending parties. Chad
was still a "worrier" and also found it difficult to leave things undone, such as
school assignments, video games, and repairs on his car. He would stay up late
completing these tasks to the detriment of his sleep.

At the age of twenty-two and while working at his first job after college,
Chad's parents divorced, and he moved in with his father. He began to
have intrusive, terrifying thoughts about killing the family dog. This fear
spread to other vulnerable targets, such as children and frail older adults.
Chad thought he was going crazy and believed himself to be an evil person.
He could not let go of the thoughts, and they made him extremely anxious.
Sleep was difficult, although Chad craved it, and he quit his job because he
was totally preoccupied by these thoughts of harm. He seldom saw friends
and began staying home for fear he would harm someone. Common stressors became entangled in obsessions as well; for example, when his com-
puter crashed, he worried obsessively about getting it fixed. Chad was
constantly anxious and felt exhausted all the time. He felt he had to do
something or he would "go out of his mind." A friend suggested that he
might be suffering from OCD, and Chad reluctantly sought help, fearing he
would be "put away." Following an assessment, he was referred to an intensive outpatient program, which definitively diagnosed the OCD, social phobia, and generalized anxiety disorder.

## THE SPECIFIC DISORDERS

This section presents an overview of the anxiety disorders so that you will
gain a familiarity with them in terms of epidemiology and etiology. The specific criteria for the disorders will be presented in Chapter 6.

### Generalized Anxiety Disorder

The focus in generalized anxiety disorder (GAD) is on negative events and is diffuse. People with GAD find themselves anxious about a wide variety of topics, such as the minor things in their lives, as well as finances, health, the future, the world, and the environment. Their thinking is characterized by threat-laden future forecasts in the unrealistic hope of making life less unpredictable and uncontrollable. They are anxious most of the time and have trouble sleeping, concentrating, and relaxing. Ruminations about the past and the future are common.

### Specific Phobias

A specific phobia involves the fear of a particular object or situation. Typical examples include heights, small spaces, spiders, snakes, dogs, and blood-injection-injury fears. People with a specific phobia avoid confronting the object of their fear. When they cannot avoid the object, they are anxious prior to contact and experience heightened physiological arousal upon encountering the object.

### Panic Disorder and Agoraphobia

A panic attack is a sudden, intense experience of fear. Possible symptoms include rapid and shallow breathing, rapid heart rate, flushing, nausea, tingling, trembling, chest pain or discomfort, and a sensation of being out of control. People often fear that they are dying or "going crazy." Agoraphobia is anxiety about, or avoidance of, places where a person may feel trapped if he or she experiences a panic attack or panic-like symptoms.

### Obsessive-Compulsive Disorder

Obsessive-compulsive disorder (OCD) is characterized by obsessions (unwanted intrusive thoughts or images that cause anxiety) and/or compulsions (ritual behaviors that are performed and may be repeated in the service of reducing anxiety). Examples of obsessions and compulsions include fear of contamination and the ritual of repetitive and prolonged handwashing, fear of leaving an appliance on or a door unlocked and the ritual of checking, and the fear of some unforeseen bad event occurring and the ritual of repeatedly reciting words, prayers, or numbers.

### Social Phobia (Social Anxiety)

Social phobia may be generalized or specific and is the fear of being evaluated or embarrassed in social or performance situations. The most common specific social phobia is the fear of public speaking. Generalized social phobia involves a wide range of social situations in which a person experiences significant anxiety, which may lead to avoidance.

### Posttraumatic Stress Disorder and Acute Stress Disorder

When people experience traumatic events, they may respond with acute stress disorder (ASD) or posttraumatic stress disorder (PTSD). The experiences are similar, but the time frames differ. ASD is a more immediate and short-term reaction that lasts two days to four weeks and occurs within four weeks of the event. On the other hand, PTSD tends to be chronic, lasting at least one month and usually longer. The onset may be well after the occurrence of the event. Both disorders involve a re-experiencing of the event when "triggered" by memories and stimuli reminiscent of the original trauma. The reliving of the trauma manifests itself in dreams and flashbacks, which are intense sensory and physiological experiences of the event. There is often a flattening of affect and an emotional distancing from other people. The fear reaction is intense and unpleasant, and it often leads to avoidance of many situations and interactions. Patients who suffer from these disorders often experience insomnia, difficulty concentrating, irritability, and hypervigilance.

## EPIDEMIOLOGY: HOW MANY OF US DEVELOP ANXIETY DISORDERS?

### The Studies

Numerous attempts have been made to determine the percentage of the population that suffers from mental disorders. Researchers in the past have been limited by vague and differing diagnostic criteria, which made it difficult to compare and aggregate studies. In addition, it is very costly to interview a huge representative sample that would yield useful and reliable data. In the United States, beginning in 1980, the Epidemiological Catchment Area Study (ECA) was launched by the U.S. National Institute of Mental Health (NIMH) following the 1977 report of the President's Commission on Mental Health. The study was recommended to assess the prevalence and incidence of mental disorders to assist in planning services for people suffering from mental health problems. Prevalence is the ratio for a given time period (one year in most epidemiological studies) of the number of occurrences of a disease compared with the number of people in the population. Incidence, or lifetime prevalence, is the number of cases of a disease to occur in the lifetime of the subjects, again, as compared with the general population.

For the ECA, five different sites were chosen in the United States, and five universities worked with the NIMH to select samples and conduct the interviews. The NIMH Diagnostic Interview Schedule (DIS), Version III, which incorporates the criteria of the *Diagnostic and Statistical Manual of Mental Disorders*, third edition (*DSM-III*), was used across all sites. Ultimately, 20,861 subjects participated.

Another large epidemiological study was begun in the early 1990s and is continuing today. The baseline National Comorbidity Survey (NCS), which was again funded by the NIMH, was originally conducted from the fall of 1990 to the spring of 1992 and used the World Health Organization Composite International Diagnostic Interview (CIDI). The CIDI was designed by using the *DSM-III Revised* (*DSM-III-R*) criteria to assess the prevalences and comorbidity of *DSM-III-R* disorders. Comorbidity refers to the co-occurrence of disorders within the same individual. This study sampled people who were in treatment for mental health problems and those who were not. Additional NCS studies reevaluated the original subjects (NCS-2), replicated the original study with a new national sample of ten thousand subjects and additional variables (NCS-R), and interviewed and studied ten thousand adolescents (NCS-A).

### Anxiety Disorders: Single Largest Mental Health Problem in the United States

The conclusion drawn from both the ECA and NCS data is that anxiety disorders are the single largest mental health problem in the United States. (It is notable that this was the finding from the ECA data even though the study did not include the diagnoses of PTSD and OCD.) For women, the most common diagnosis is specific phobia; for men, specific phobia is the second most common diagnosis, and alcohol abuse and alcohol dependence are the most common. The NCS-R study reported that nearly seventy-five percent of those with an anxiety disorder will have their first episode by age twenty-one. Another finding revealed that anxiety disorders are chronic illnesses. Untreated depressive episodes, on average, last no more than nine months, whereas anxiety disorders, even when treated, generally persist throughout one's life. The rates of disorder reported in the NCS-R study are shown in Tables 4.1 and 4.2.

### Global Assessment of the Prevalence of Anxiety Disorders

Between 2001 and 2003, a survey was conducted by the World Health Organization in fourteen developed and developing nations in Europe, Asia, Africa, the Middle East, and the Americas to assess the prevalence of mental health

**Table 4.1**
**Percentage of the total U.S. population suffering from mental disorders[1]**

| Disorders | 12-month prevalence (%) | Lifetime prevalence (%)[2] |
|---|---|---|
| **Most prevalent disorders** | | |
| Specific phobia | 8.7 | |
| Social phobia | 6.8 | |
| Major depressive disorder | 6.7 | |
| **Most prevalent disorders by class** | | |
| Anxiety disorders | 18.1 | 28.8 |
| Mood disorders | 9.5 | 20.8 |
| Impulse-control disorders | 8.9 | 24.8 |
| Substance abuse disorders | 3.8 | 14.8 |
| **Any anxiety disorder by sex[3]** | | |
| Men | 11.8 | 19.2 |
| Women | 22.6 | 30.5 |

[1]*Source:* Kessler, Chiu et al. 2005.
[2]*Sources:* Kessler, Bergland et al. 2005.
[3]*Source:* Kessler et al. 1994.

problems worldwide. The study revealed that anxiety disorders plague the human race more than any other mental disorder. Rates vary from country to country, with the United States having the highest incidence of anxiety disorders in the world. Anxiety rates were also high in France, Colombia, and Lebanon. China and Nigeria showed the lowest rates of anxiety disorders. The notion that anxiety disorders are a correlate of industrialization and development does not appear to be supported by these data. Germany and Spain for example, had lower rates of anxiety disorders. Although this study had several methodological problems, the findings were consistent with previous and varied surveys.

Clearly, there are a variety of cultural factors that have an impact on the incidence of anxiety disorders in a society. There is some evidence that living in truly dangerous conditions increases the incidence of GAD. Studies of people living in the area around Three Mile Island (the site of a nuclear plant accident in the United States) and those directly affected by Hurricane Katrina in 2005 showed a much higher incidence of GAD. In addition, poverty has been found to correlate with higher rates of GAD. Poverty comes with reduced job opportunities and, often, unsafe communities. In the United States, African Americans and Hispanic Americans appear to suffer from GAD more than the Caucasian population. When researchers control for poverty and joblessness among these groups, their GAD rates are comparable to those of the Caucasian population.

Table 4.2
NCS-R prevalence of individual anxiety disorders

**GAD**
- Approximately 6.8 million American adults, or about 3.1 percent of people age 18 and over, have GAD in a given year.[1]
- Approximately 5.1 percent have GAD during their lifetime.[2]

**Specific phobia**
- Approximately 19.2 million American adults age 18 and over, or about 8.7 percent of people in this age group in a given year, have some type of specific phobia.[1]
- Approximately 11.3 percent have a specific phobia during their lifetime.[2]

**Panic disorder**
- Approximately 6 million American adults ages 18 and older, or about 2.7 percent of people in this age group in a given year, have panic disorder.[1]
- Approximately 3.5 percent have panic disorder during their lifetime.[2]
- About one in three people with panic disorder develops agoraphobia, a condition in which the individual becomes afraid of being in any place or situation from which escape might be difficult or where help is unavailable in the event of a panic attack.[1]

**Agoraphobia**
- Approximately 1.8 million American adults age 18 and over, or about 0.8 percent of people in this age group in a given year, have agoraphobia without a history of panic disorder.[1]
- Approximately 5.3 percent have agoraphobia during their lifetime.[2]

**OCD**
- Approximately 2.2 million American adults age 18 and older, or about 1.0 percent of people in this age group in a given year, have OCD.[1]

**Social phobia**
- Approximately 15 million American adults age 18 and over, or about 6.8 percent of people in this age group in a given year, have social phobia.[1]
- Approximately 13.3 percent have social phobia during their lifetime.[2]

**PTSD**
- Approximately 7.7 million American adults age 18 and older, or about 3.5 percent of people in this age group in a given year, have PTSD.[1]
- About 19 percent of Vietnam veterans experienced PTSD at some point after the war.[1]
- The disorder also frequently occurs after violent personal assaults, such as rape, mugging, or domestic violence; terrorism; natural or human-caused disasters; and accidents.

[1]*Source*: Kessler, Chiu et al. 2005.
[2]*Source*: Kessler, Bergland et al. 2005.

## ETIOLOGY: HOW DO ANXIETY DISORDERS DEVELOP?

Since all humans experience fear and anxiety, what is it that causes an individual to develop an anxiety disorder? We know that the answer lies in both nature and nurture. Strong evidence supports the theory that genetic and biological components are involved in the development of these disorders. A person's environment is a complex combination of child rearing, life experiences, learning, and culture that interacts with the temperament and innate biology of the individual. This section explores the role that these factors play in the etiology of anxiety disorders.

### Genetics and Psychological Vulnerabilities

After years of studies on the inheritance of "anxiety neuroses," anxiety disorders in general, and the specific anxiety disorders, we can safely say that anxiousness or nervousness runs in families. Three areas of studies have been very significant in allowing scientists to reach the conclusion of heritability. Scientists have been able to breed into animals what they call "emotionality," which they believe is comparable to anxiety sensitivity in humans. Studies on the aspects of human personality and normal emotional experience have shown strong evidence that the personality trait of anxiety, or "neuroticism," as it had been called, is genetically transmitted. In addition, studies on the specific anxiety disorders, particularly as diagnostic criteria have become more precise, have also shown that anxiety disorders are most likely inherited.

Genetic studies are complex and time consuming. Family studies involve the interviewing of a proband, or the person identified with the disorder. The researcher may gather a family history from the proband, but this method is extremely open to error and gaps. A better method is to interview the family members directly. Generally, the inquiries are to first-degree relatives (parents, offspring, and siblings) to identify the aggregation, or collection of family members who also have the disorder. This is compared with a control group in which none of the primary subjects are diagnosed with the disorder. The rates of aggregation of the disorder within the families of the two groups are then compared. In one particularly well-done study, for example, Raymond Crowe and colleagues examined the occurrence of panic in relatives of patients hospitalized for panic disorder. The data showed that for the panic group, 24.7 percent of relatives also had the same diagnosis; for the control group, however, only 2.3 percent of the relatives had panic disorder. Additional studies have supported this finding.

Family studies are unable to control for the contribution of environmental and learning factors in the development of a mental disorder. On the other hand, studying the rates within twin groups can shed further light on the inheritance question.

Twin studies allow for the comparison of the rate of concordance between people who have identical genetic makeup and those who do not. Concordance is the presence of a given trait in both members of a pair of twins. The concordance rate of monozygotic twins, or identical twins (from one zygote or egg), is compared with the concordance rate of dizygotic twins, or fraternal twins (from two zygotes or eggs, therefore having nonidentical genetic makeup). An excellent example of this type of study was performed in Norway, where there are very good demographic records. In 1983, Sven Torgersen examined pairs in which one of the twins was identified as having panic disorder. He reported that there was a 45 percent risk of both monozygotic twins having panic disorder, whereas dizygotic twins had only a 15 percent chance of both twins having the same diagnosis. Although it is likely that twins would be raised in a similar manner, Torgersen was able to account or control for the impact of environment. He was able to conclude that there is a genetic basis for the aggregation of panic disorder in families. Most other studies of this nature have replicated his findings.

Studies have also been conducted on the heritability of specific fears and phobias. Scientists have concluded that specific phobias are most likely genetically transmitted, and evidence is pointing to the likelihood that the fear of particular objects is inherited. Collaborative research between the New York State Psychiatric Institute and Boston University is now indicating that the fear of small animals, blood-injection-injury phobia, and social phobia tend to run in families.

In addition to the studies that show that certain anxiety disorders are inherited, a growing body of evidence suggests that there is genetic vulnerability to developing anxiety disorders in general. This is called a nonspecific genetic contribution for anxiety. Kenneth Kendler, a behavioral geneticist now at Virginia Commonwealth University, has supported this conclusion through research. In addition, researchers are finding what appears to be a genetic physiological component that underlies both anxiety disorders and the personality trait of nervousness. In 1967, Hans Eysenck proposed that an overactive autonomic nervous system was the underlying biological factor in anxiety vulnerability. Scientists have since accumulated additional evidence supporting the notion that the autonomic nervous system, as well as other brain-regulated systems, are involved in the genetically determined vulnerability to nervousness and anxiety disorders. This physiological or biological vulnerability may also underlie "stress disorders" such as hypertension (high blood pressure) and anger. These physiological stress disorders often occur without the experience of anxiety.

Kendler and other researchers believe that anxiety disorders are most likely derived from multiple genes (polygenic) and are located on a variety of chromosomal areas. In addition, Kendler and his colleagues also found that GAD and major depressive disorder seem to have a common genetic source.

In his review of genetic studies of anxiety disorders, David Barlow has observed that the findings are leading to a conclusion that both genetics (nature) and environment (nurture) play a role in the development of anxiety disorders. The belief is that a genetic predisposition, or diathesis, for anxiety, plus environmental stress (psychological vulnerabilities) will lead to the expression of the disorder. This is a stress-diathesis model for the development of a disorder.

A biological vulnerability to anxiety alone does not usually "make" an anxiety disorder. Research indicates that early life experiences, such as actual stressful events, a generally stressful environment, or parental modeling, create a general psychological vulnerability. A third vulnerability that most likely contributes to focal fears (as in phobias, panic, OCD, and PTSD) is a specific negative event, which can be a solitary occurrence or a repeated negative experience (such as ongoing physical abuse or a parent who models an extreme fear of spiders). This third vulnerability is called a specific psychological vulnerability.

Studies of psychological resilience point to possible protective factors that can mitigate against the development of an anxiety disorder. Coping skills, good familial supports, and an internal locus of control contribute to the development of psychological hardiness. Locus of control, measured in degrees of internal or external control, refers to the perceived amount of personal control one has in life. Research has shown that an internal locus of control is fostered by warm, consistent, sensitive, and contingent (natural and logical behavioral consequences) parenting. In addition, parental encouragement of independence, problem solving, and skill development also contributes to an internal locus of control. The resilience literature also indicates that having a stable, caring adult attachment (even outside the family) helps children deal effectively with adversity and stressors that could contribute to the development of anxiety disorders.

As medical science and biological science advance in the area of genetics, scientists can further investigate the genes that are responsible for the development of certain traits or disorders. Promising data are emerging from the research on specific genes in the etiology of mental disorders in general and anxiety specifically. The enzyme catechol-O-methyltransferase (COMT) plays a significant role in the regulation of neurotransmitters, including dopamine and norepinephrine, especially in the prefrontal cortex of the brain. The prefrontal cortex is responsible for executive functioning, which involves

## A Legacy of Anxiety

Catherine had her first panic attack when she went away to college. She grew up with an anxious father and a mother who drank excessively. Catherine had always attributed her nervousness to growing up with an unpredictable mother and a high-strung father, who was constantly trying to manage the fallout from his wife's drinking and neglect of the children. The panic attack prompted Catherine to seek help.

As Catherine researched panic disorder, she also came to understand her own history of anxiety in a different way. Her life at home had indeed been stressful, but her father was able to tell her that she had exhibited signs of anxiety even as a toddler, when the family environment had been calmer. He himself had always been nervous. Catherine also learned that her mother suffered from severe social phobia and likely drank to find relief from her anxiety. A study of her family tree (genogram) led to other discoveries.

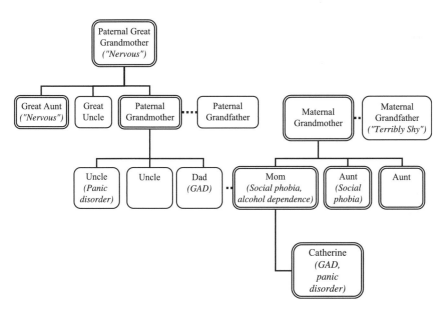

**Figure 4.1** A genogram of Catherine's family shows a history of anxiety disorders in both her maternal and paternal lines. Male relatives appear in single-lined boxes, and female relatives appear in double-lined boxes.

planning, inhibition of behaviors, abstract thinking, emotion, personality, and working memory. This part of the brain synthesizes and organizes information from other regions of the brain. A change in the composition of the COMT enzyme, caused by a variation of the gene that encodes it, makes the processing of both cognition and emotion inefficient. Researchers are studying this variation as a possible factor for panic disorder, GAD, OCD, and other mental disorders. The COMT gene could function in relation to other genes and the environment to produce the full expression of a disorder.

## Models of Etiology of Specific Anxiety Disorders

The underlying assumption in the development of all anxiety disorders is the synergy that is created when the nonspecific biological vulnerability and the general and sometimes specific psychological vulnerabilities come together. It is believed that the specific psychological vulnerabilities may determine the particular anxiety disorder or depressive disorder that is manifested.

### GAD

GAD is thought of as the "basic" anxiety disorder. Although the median (middle) age of onset for GAD is thirty-one years old, GAD can begin at any point in a person's life. The experience of GAD is pervasive and chronic.

As vulnerabilities and stressful life events come together, the physiological response of negative emotional affect ensues, and a shift occurs in attention from the issue at hand to self-evaluation ("How am I doing? Is this the right thing to do? Oh, I am so anxious. What if ...?"). The person becomes hypervigilant, and there is interference with information processing. Negative and threat-laden cognitive assumptions are generated and maintained.

### Specific Phobias

In the etiology of phobias, there is an association of a true or false alarm with a stimulus, either an object or situation, which runs the risk of becoming sufficiently distressing to be considered a phobia. The high emotional reactivity that is part of the genetic physiological vulnerability allows for intense emotional learning or conditioning, so that the object or situation becomes feared in advance (anxious apprehension) and is reacted to with both cognitive and physiological responses. The person acquires a fear response to the conditioned stimulus. The anxiety in phobia, and panic disorder for that matter, is essentially fear of fear. As a result of a psychological vulnerability, the person fears the alarm reaction to the stimulus and often avoids the object or situation, which reinforces the fear. A specific phobia usually begins in child-hood; the median age of onset is seven years.

In 1976, S.J. Rachman proposed three possible routes to acquiring a phobia: direct experience of an event (direct conditioning), vicarious or observational learning, and informational learning. Subsequent research has supported these possible pathways. Barlow and colleague Martin Antony have suggested that there are additional factors that mitigate for or against the development of phobias. These factors include previous exposure to the feared situation, subse-quent exposure to the feared situation (getting back on the horse that threw you), and prior learning. The context of the situation, such as an individual's level of stress at the time of the event, and the perception of control over the event are also factors.

### Panic Disorder

In people who develop panic disorder, the general biological vulnerability to anxiety is evidenced by a marked physiological reaction. In addition, there is some evidence pointing to specific heritability for reacting to stress with panic attacks. People with panic disorder experience false alarms that are the fight-or-flight fear reaction of the autonomic nervous system. The factors con-tributing to the development of an anxiety disorder are the psychological vul-nerabilities that incline the person experiencing a false alarm to experience and interpret it as dangerous and, ultimately, to fear its reoccurrence. Anxious apprehension and internal focus then escalate the physiological response and increase its frequency. On the basis of learning and early experiences, the per-son may then begin to avoid situations where he or she is fearful of having a panic attack or situations that are associated with the false alarm. The escala-tion may result in agoraphobia. Some patients also avoid activities that induce physiological experiences typical of a panic attack for fear that the activity will actually bring on a panic attack, such as avoiding climbing stairs because of the resultant increase in heart rate. Panic disorder typically begins in early adulthood, but the age of onset can occur at any point throughout adulthood. The median age of onset for panic disorder is twenty-four, and the median age of onset of agoraphobia (with or without panic) is twenty.

### OCD

Observations of animal behavior have shown scientists that some animals engage in ritual and stereotyped behaviors when under stress. It is believed that this tendency is innate. People who develop OCD have a physiological and psychological genetic vulnerability to respond to stress in a highly emotional manner. All people experience intrusive thoughts; however, people with OCD experience these thoughts with high negative affect and physiological stress, find them unacceptable, and come to fear them. The thoughts become unpredictable and uncontrollable. The more the patient tries to avoid or suppress the thoughts, the more the anxiety and distress intensify. It becomes a vicious cycle and, as is typical in anxiety disorders, the person's attentional focus narrows. The obsessional beliefs are inflexible, even though the individual knows them to be extreme or illogical. A standard theme in the symptomatology of OCD is the inability to trust one's experience, landing it the early name "the doubting disease." Patients with OCD clearly make persistent cognitive errors. Research indicates that interference in cognitive processing (specifically in the areas of categorizing, organizing, and having the ability to shift a mental set) plays a role in OCD. The first symptoms of OCD often begin during childhood or adolescence; however, the median age of onset for the full disorder is nineteen.

Gail Steketee and other researchers studying the etiology of the specific content of obsessions are finding that parental style or parental OCD symptoms seem to affect the symptom picture of their children. It has been my observation in clinical practice that this is sometimes accurate, but I have also found other correlates with symptom content. Sometimes symptoms relate to what is salient at the particular time of life of the patient, such as obsessions about sexual identity or social issues in adolescence. I find that many school-age children and teens with OCD obsess about the perfection of their school work and, as a result, reread and rewrite their assignments. OCD is often exacerbated by the stress of pregnancy and childbirth, and many new mothers with OCD obsess about their children's or their own safety or fear they will kill their child. For some patients, the content of their obsessions seems symbolic of early trauma or is an attempt to protect against earlier trauma. On occasion, the content of obsessions and compulsion does not appear to have any particular trigger or symbolism in the patient's life at all. Symptoms can also fluctuate over the course of the illness, with some disappearing and others taking their place.

### Social Phobia (Social Anxiety Disorder)

Like patients with other anxiety disorders, patients with social phobia experience physiological and cognitive reactions and may or may not come to avoid anxiety-provoking situations. Besides the general biological vulnerability necessary for the development of an anxiety disorder, there appear to be other possible genetic precursors to social phobia. Humans may have a biological readiness to react fearfully when confronted by angry or critical eye contact. Primates use direct eye contact to intimidate a foe or rival. Since humans have a more complex response to eye contact than other primates, social anxiety may be an exaggerated response to some basic wariness of angry, critical gazing. In social phobia, patients fear critical evaluation, and evidence now shows that socially phobic people respond more negatively than others to critical faces.

There seem to be different pathways in the development of social phobia. Other heritable traits that seem to contribute to social phobia are shyness and behavioral inhibition. Shyness is one of the most heritable personality traits and correlates highly with social phobia. In addition, behavioral inhibition, which is expressed in children through timidity, fearfulness, and wariness, is also a temperament that is genetically transmitted. The exact relationship of these factors is not known, but they have a clear connection to social phobia.

People with specific social phobias can usually point to a precipitating event that triggered an alarm similar to a panic attack. They are fearful of experiencing this physiological arousal the next time they are in that situation. According to Richard Heimberg, a possible key psychological vulnerability to generalized social phobia is being raised by parents who are hypercritical and evaluative. Interestingly, these parents likely suffer from their own social anxiety. Retrospective studies (based on the subjects' reports of their upbringing) have shown the tendency of socially phobic people to perceive their parents as rejecting, overprotective, unaccepting, and emotionally distant. Social phobia begins in childhood or adolescence, with a median age of onset of thirteen.

People with generalized social phobia tend to have more diffuse anxiety responses, rather than panic attacks, to a wide variety of situations. Both groups of people fear embarrassment, and both groups experience cognitive interference from their racing cognitions and internal self-focus. Research done by Heimberg and his colleagues has indicated that the self-focused attention in social phobia disrupts performance. This disruption reinforces the person's beliefs and fears and frequently prompts avoidance and maintains the disorder.

## PTSD

PTSD is an interesting disorder because it involves a clear precipitating event that triggers the onset of the disorder. In addition, there is a unique set of symptoms that involve the re-experiencing of the traumatic event in dreams, flashbacks, and physiological alarms. Much of the early research on PTSD was focused on soldiers who had been in combat and who experienced horrific events. Not everyone who experiences horrific events, such as accidents, rape, combat, or abuse, develops PTSD. Again, there appears to be a biological pre-disposition for developing PTSD when confronted with a traumatic event. However, it has been noted by researchers looking at the impact of torture on U.S. prisoners of war that at some point the events become so brutal and pro-longed that all victims are affected psychologically. The severity of the trauma can therefore diminish the role of biological vulnerability. The intensity of the event, the proximity of exposure to the event, and the number of exposures (for example, in the case of child abuse) affect the severity and the likelihood of developing the disorder.

Researchers have found that a variety of events can contribute to the develop-ment of PTSD. In addition to combat, other events include physical and sexual assault, car accidents, natural and human-caused disasters, witnessing or being the victim of a crime, and the death of a child. The NCS study yielded data that have deepened our understanding of some of the factors involved in the inci-dence of PTSD. The data show that combat and rape are the events most likely to induce the disorder, yet the event that most commonly produces PTSD is the sudden death of a loved one. The data also show that women are more than twice as likely to develop PTSD as men (10.4 percent of women had a lifetime inci-dence of PTSD, whereas only 5.0 percent of men reported a history of the disor-der). A study of Vietnam veterans shows that there is a differential lifetime incidence among European Americans (14 percent), African Americans (21 per-cent), and Hispanic Americans (28 percent). Some of the variance can be attrib-uted to different levels of exposure to combat; however, there is still a significant difference even when the rates of exposure are considered. Other studies have shown the same trend. Researchers continue to investigate the factors involved in this differential expression of the disorder. Certain risk factors may play a role in the vulnerability to PTSD. Studies have shown that prior exposure to trau-matic events, an unstable family environment, and the stress level at the time of and after the exposure are contributing factors.

The development of PTSD follows the stress-diathesis path that is common with other anxiety disorders and has a distinct precipitating event. Family studies show that a general genetic predisposition to anxiety sensitivity is a likely con-tributing factor. Victims of PTSD tend to have a higher incidence of family mem-bers who have a psychiatric disorder. Psychological vulnerability and coping skills also play a part in the likelihood of experiencing PTSD. The development of PTSD is a clear case of classical conditioning in which the victim experiences a true alarm of great intensity, which is the basic emotion of fear. The fear may be mixed with rage and distress and becomes a learned response to any stimuli that relate to or resemble the traumatic event. These may include physiological cues, memories of the event, and the event's anniversary. Anxious apprehension develops when the person fears experiencing the learned alarm, and emotional numbing may occur as a protective response. Patients believe that the world is dangerously unpredictable and fear that they cannot control events and emotional reactions. The anxiety response is maintained by avoidance of any cues of the event. PTSD can develop at any age, including childhood, but research shows that the median age of onset is twenty-three years.

Certain protective factors apparently help guard against the development of PTSD. Researchers have found that the older people are when exposed to a traumatic event, especially men, the less likely it is that they will develop the disorder. In addition, people who are married are less likely to experience PTSD. In general, having a good support network seems to be protective. In addition, it has been found that a person is less likely to develop PTSD when he or she has the opportunity to be exposed to the same circumstance or stimuli shortly after the event without another occurrence of the trauma. An example of this would be to return to the site of a physical or sexual assault or a car accident.

## COMORBIDITY

Comorbidity is the co-occurrence of medical conditions and has implications for severity of functioning, treatment, disease course, and chronicity. Patients with comorbid mental disorders tend to be more disabled, and the prognoses for treatment outcomes are less favorable than for those with one disorder. Comorbidity increases utilization of medical services, the presence of other medical problems, suicide risk, and loss of work productivity. It also has implications for treatment. For example, when dealing with anxiety patients with addictions, it is necessary to address the addiction before other treatment can be effective. If the anxiety is not addressed, however, it may be difficult for patients to maintain sobriety if they have used substances to self-medicate the anxiety symptoms. In addition, if the person's drug of choice was a central nervous system (CNS) depressant, such as alcohol, the use of benzodiazepines, which are also CNS depressants, would be contraindicated because of the risk of further addiction. Treatment becomes more complicated.

The NCS results show that nearly half (45 percent) of those with any mental disorder meet criteria for two or more disorders. For anxiety disorders, this figure is even higher; somewhere between 50 and 55 percent have at least one additional disorder, with a rate as high as 76 percent for lifetime prevalence. Patients with a principal diagnosis of an anxiety disorder are most likely to have a comorbid diagnosis of another anxiety disorder, a depressive disorder, and/or substance abuse. The likelihood of someone having another *DSM* Axis

I (mental disorder) or Axis II (personality disorder) diagnosis varies significantly with the principal diagnosis. The most common anxiety disorders to have at least one other diagnosis are PTSD (88.3 percent of men and 79.0 percent of women have an additional disorder) and OCD (80 percent of all patients have a depressive disorder). Specific phobia is the least likely anxiety disorder to have a comorbid diagnosis.

PTSD is complex in its relationship to other disorders. It has the highest comorbidity rate for at least one additional diagnosis among anxiety disorders, and multiple diagnoses are very common among those with PTSD. According to the NCS data, 59 percent of men and 44 percent of women with PTSD have three or more diagnoses. More than half of all patients with PTSD also have an alcohol abuse or dependence problem. This rate is even higher when those who abuse prescription and illegal drugs are included. In addition to drug and alcohol problems, many patients with PTSD develop anxiety disorders and depression. An estimated 20 percent of those with PTSD have attempted suicide. An Australian study (National Mental Health and Well-Being Survey) found that 62 percent of patients with PTSD had experienced suicidal ideation (thoughts of suicide).

Frequently, victims of PTSD have a preexisting psychiatric disorder. It is known that a preexisting anxiety or mood disorder is a risk factor for the development of PTSD. In addition, certain disorders, such as panic, depression, conduct disorder, antisocial personality disorder, and social anxiety, can lead to the use of addictive substances. The use of illegal drugs and alcohol increases the likelihood of exposure to violent events and consequently raises the chances of developing PTSD.

People with GAD or panic disorder have a high incidence of physical ailments and are high users of primary medical care. Those with panic disorder utilize emergency services more and are seven times as likely to be hospitalized as the general population. Chest pain, respiratory complaints, and gastrointestinal problems are common to sufferers of GAD and panic. There is a high correlation of GAD with migraine disorder and irritable bowel syndrome (IBS). There is no disease process with IBS; rather it is a stress-related, functional disorder in which the large intestine does not work properly. Patients complain of gas, urgency, cramping, constipation, and diarrhea. IBS can be a debilitating, life-altering condition.

As discussed earlier, anxiety disorders and depressive disorders have an interesting relationship. The two disorders share the symptoms of restlessness, agitation, fatigue, difficulty concentrating, insomnia, and changes in appetite. According to Barlow, the discriminating symptoms between the two disorders are those specific to depression: motor retardation (lethargy), hopelessness, depressed mood, and suicidal thoughts.

In addition to common symptomatology, anxiety and depression frequently co-occur. Some patients clearly meet criteria for both a depressive and an anxiety disorder, and there are those who meet the criteria for a major depressive episode and have many features of anxiety. Although these descriptions are not in the *DSM*, clinicians and researchers have referred to "anxious depression" and "neurotic depression" to describe those depressive episodes. There is a movement toward making this experience of mixed depression and anxiety its own diagnostic category in *DSM-V*.

Approximately 50 to 70 percent of all anxiety disorder patients, currently or in their lifetime, also suffer from a depressive disorder. Frequently, the anxiety disorder occurs prior to the onset of the depressive disorder. Suffering from a severe anxiety disorder can increase one's sense of hopelessness and frustration over time and lead to depression. The combination of depression and anxiety increases the rate of suicide attempts and completion.

Biologically, the same neurotransmitters have been implicated in both anxiety and depression: dopamine, norepinephrine, and serotonin. This conclusion was drawn from the finding that the antidepressants (monoamine oxidase inhibitors, tricyclics, and selective serotonin reuptake inhibitors) are often effective in relieving anxiety symptoms. Additional studies have led to the reasoning that anxiety and depression share a similar neurochemistry and neurocircuitry. The findings of Kendler and other researchers point to a shared biological vulnerability. Anxiety and depressive disorders tend to cluster in families, and the belief is that psychological vulnerabilities determine which disorder will be expressed.

There are also cognitive processing similarities between the two disorders. Studies have shown that both groups tend to engage in automatic cognitive processing that results in negative thoughts. These often distorted thoughts contribute to a lack of perspective in both anxious and depressed persons. It appears that nonanxious and nondepressed individuals usually engage in more controlled information processing and are more able to reflect upon the accuracy of their thoughts. Neither the depressed individual with pessimistic views of self, future, and the world nor the anxious individual with exaggerated views of threat and danger tends to question the reality or accuracy of his or her perspective, which may contribute to the maintenance or exacerbation of both disorders.

Because of the complicated clinical picture of patients with comorbid disorders, it is essential to assess the presence of all disorders, including physical disorders and especially depression and substance abuse or dependence. The chronology of disorders should be carefully assessed before an effective treatment plan can be designed.

## CULTURAL DIFFERENCES IN THE MANIFESTATION OF ANXIETY DISORDERS

The expression of symptoms and the explanations for anxiety disorders differ in various cultures. Barlow points out that even within Western culture, the expression of emotion and anxiety is different. For example, southern and Mediterranean Europeans are known for their intensity of emotional expression, whereas northern Europeans tend to be more reserved. Different cultures have different coping skills, rituals, and outlets for expressions of anxiety.

OCD has symptoms that differ between cultures. For example, studies show that Saudi patients with OCD are much more likely to have religious obsessions than any other cultural group. It has been observed that there is a greater percentage of people in Saudi Arabia who practice their religion compared with other cultures. The content and manifestation of obsessions and compulsions in a culture will be focused on concerns that are familiar and salient to people within that culture.

In Chinese culture, there are several phobias that exist specific to the concept of *yin* and *yang*. *Pa-Leng* is known as frigophobia, or fear of the cold. Sufferers fear that an overabundance of yin, which is the cold, dark, windy aspect of life, will rob them of bodily warmth and, ultimately, their life. They wear layers of clothing to keep them warm even on hot days. Another feared result of the overabundance of yin is what is called *koro*. Koro is the fear that one's genitals will retract into the body and lead to death. Other societies, such as some cultures in Latin America and the Caribbean, still hold to the belief of spiritual causes of anxiety disorders. They consider black magic or witchcraft to be the basis for suffering, and the remedies are in accordance with those beliefs. It has also been observed in some of the above-mentioned cultures that the focus on and experience of some physiological symptoms are different. Some cultures have an incidence of conversion disorders (such as limb paralysis or blindness without organic cause) and hallucinations associated with panic disorder, which are not typical of most other cultures. Researchers have indicated that African Americans have a higher incidence of hypertension with panic disorder than European or Hispanic Americans.

Because of the differential presentation and understanding of anxiety disorders, the assessing and treating clinician must pay particular attention to cultural factors and work within patients' belief systems to a certain extent. Even among mainstream culture patients in the United States, Canada, and the United Kingdom, it is important to assess the understanding of anxiety disorders and their etiology. Many people continue to hold Freudian assumptions about the origin of anxiety disorders, see their disorder as a weakness, and sometimes try to "tough it out." Education is a key component of treatment. It is important that people understand the genetic and psychosocial aspects of their anxiety disorders and realize that they are not alone in their suffering. It is amazing how many patients are relieved to find out that there are many others who experience anxiety with such intensity. People so often assume that everyone else "has it all together." Many people with anxiety disorders have become masters at showing the world a calm demeanor.

# 5

# The Biology of Anxiety Disorders

 e now know, without question, that the symptoms of anxiety disorders originate in the brain. Ever since the classical Greeks recognized that the brain was the seat of thought and emotion, scientists have sought to understand how the brain functions in our experience of emotion and psychiatric disorders. Accepted theories concerning the importance of the brain have varied throughout history. Twentieth- and twenty-first-century scientists have built on the findings of those before them and greatly advanced our knowledge of the brain and its workings.

Walter Cannon's study of emotion in the 1920s initiated a trend in the study of anxiety disorders. He proposed that emotion is primarily a brain function. Early animal research in this area involved the removal of parts of the brain to determine the regions most likely implicated in emotion. Cannon discovered that the cerebral cortex served a controlling function for emotions, which were generated in the hypothalamus region of the brain. Later researchers expanded Cannon's work and deduced that the limbic system of the brain is actively involved in emotional experience and expression (see Figure 5.1). This is a very primitive part of the brain and is responsible for emotional life and the formation of memories. These brain structures serve similar functions in other mammals.

Advances in neuroscience led to the technique of electrical stimulation of parts of the human brain to determine the structures involved in specific emotional responses. As the century progressed, attention focused on the role of neurotransmitters, and research led to a more comprehensive picture of the brain structures and processes in anxiety disorders. Research continues in these areas, and new knowledge is being gained in leaps and bounds as more sophisticated techniques, such as brain imaging, are developed.

## NEUROBIOLOGY

Empirical evidence has supported the idea that anxiety is a complicated neurobiological occurrence. Activation of the limbic system affects cortical (having to do with the cerebral cortex) and autonomic nervous system (ANS) arousal, the experience of anxiety, and therefore anxiety disorders. The genetic vulnerability for anxiety disorders contributes to the level of reactivity of cortical and autonomic systems. Patients with anxiety disorders have high resting levels of cortical arousal and autonomic system reactivity.

### The Autonomic Nervous System

The ANS is responsible for regulation of the basic visceral (organ) processes needed for the maintenance of normal bodily functions. Stress, fear, sexual excitement, and alterations in the sleep-wakefulness cycle change the level of autonomic activity. The ANS affects the heart, muscles, and endocrine system and also channels visceral sensory information to the central nervous system in a feedback mechanism to adjust ANS activity appropriately. The ANS also causes the release of certain hormones, such as norepinephrine, which is crucial to the fight-or-flight response. There are three major components of the ANS: the sympathetic nervous system (SNS), which is responsible for visceral activation and the fight-or-flight response; the parasympathetic nervous system (PNS), which is responsible for calming the body and returning it to homeostasis; and the enteric nervous system, which is involved in digestion. Stimulation of the SNS causes the pupils to dilate; increases heart rate, glucose production (for energy), norepinephrine and epinephrine secretion, and blood flow to large muscle groups; and decreases digestion and bowel and bladder activity. It also relaxes the bronchial muscles to allow for increased and deeper respiration. The PNS serves the opposite function of returning the body to its relaxed state by lowering heart rate and respiration, resuming digestion, and resuming bowel and bladder function.

## The Limbic System

The limbic system is responsible for functions necessary to the survival of the organism and the species, the generation of emotions, and the formation of memories. It is the feeling and reacting part of the brain, which processes anxiety-related information. The major structures of the limbic system are the hypothalamus, hippocampus, amygdala, the pituitary gland, and the cingulate gyrus. The hypothalamus regulates hunger and thirst, plus the responses to pain, pleasure, sexual stimuli, fear, anger, and aggression. It is the major structure that regulates the functioning of the SNS and PNS. The hypothalamus is responsible for endocrine function and is connected to the pituitary gland, which in turn releases hormones into the bloodstream and affects the rest of the endocrine system. The hippocampus attaches emotional significance to memories and converts short-term memories into long-term memories. It is also involved in the retrieval of memories.

The amygdala coordinates behavioral, autonomic, and endocrine responses to stimuli with emotional content, especially fear and anxiety. It functions as an early warning system and does not discriminate stimuli well. A central purpose of the amygdala apparently is to detect threats to the organism; consequently, it plays a huge role in anxiety disorders. Other parts of the limbic system function to sort out dangerous from nondangerous stimuli. The prefrontal cortex is responsible for executive functioning: decision making, planning, abstract thought, and logic. It has been observed that prefrontal cortical activity seems to regulate and restrain emotion-related structures, especially the amygdala. When prefrontal cortical activation is low, the activity of the amygdala is heightened, leading to unpredictable eruptions of emotion, particularly anxiety and panic. In addition, it has been discovered that there are two pathways through the amygdala. One pathway processes information from the thalamus into the amygdala without cerebral cortex involvement. This induces an immediate fear reaction, without thinking. The second pathway processes information from the thalamus through the cerebral cortex and then to the amygdala. This allows for the retrieval of memories regarding the threat, thus leading to a more thoughtful response, or possibly a conditioned-fear response in people with an anxiety disorder. There is also speculation that the first pathway is the default pathway for some anxiety disorders.

The cingulate gyrus provides a pathway from the thalamus (which lies between the cerebral cortex and the midbrain structures of the limbic system) to the hippocampus; it coordinates sensory input with emotions and seems to be responsible for focusing attention on emotionally significant events. It is implicated in obsessive-compulsive disorder (OCD).

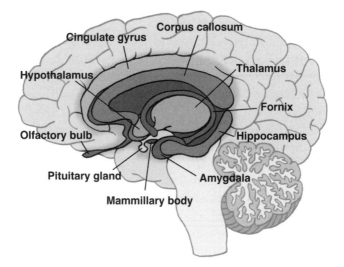

**Figure 5.1** Sagittal section of the brain showing the primary structures of the limbic system. (Courtesy of Anil Shukla)

Other structures related to the limbic system that are involved in anxiety disorders are the basal ganglia, or basal nuclei. This collection of nuclei, or nerve cells, is found on both sides of the thalamus, outside and above the limbic system, and is also connected to the cerebral cortex. The basal ganglia are situated below the cingulate gyrus. The important neurotransmitters involved with the basal ganglia are the inhibitory neurotransmitter gamma-amino butyric acid (GABA) and glutamate. The basal ganglia are important in the functioning of motor control and coordination, cognition, speech, and learning. They have been found to be involved in OCD and Tourette's and tic disorders, as well as movement disorders such as Parkinson's disease. Since abnormally high levels of glutamate are found in those suffering from OCD, current research is examining the possibility of glutamate-reducing medications being used to remedy this anxiety disorder.

### The Role of Brain Function in Anxiety Disorders

David Barlow, in his review of the literature on brain functioning in anxiety disorders (*Anxiety and Its Disorders: The Nature and Treatment of Anxiety and Panic*), reports that there are two sets of findings that have received growing consensus among neuroscientists and a third set of findings that shows further promise of helping us understand brain function in disorders of anxiety. Elevated sympathetic activity, autonomic inflexibility, and asymmetrical patterns of brain activity are all associated with anxiety disorders.

### Elevated Sympathetic Activity

Scientists have discovered that patients with anxiety disorders, except for those with specific phobia, have overly active SNSs. This elevated sympathetic activity leaves patients in a state of chronic overarousal. Physiological findings include such indicators as a higher resting heart rate and differences in bowel activity (thought to be related to irritable bowel syndrome), as well as increased brain-wave activity indicating a less relaxed state. Anxious patients return to a relaxed state less quickly than nonanxious people after repeated exposure to stressful events. Scientists have been able to isolate the neuromechanism involved with "toughening up" (developing increased resistance to stress) and recognize that it is the same process that occurs with treatment with serotonergic antidepressants and exposure-based therapy. Essentially, people with anxiety disorders have "the volume turned up" relative to anxiety-producing stimuli and do not "toughen up" without help as is more typical with nonanxious people.

### Autonomic Inflexibility

Another robust finding for anxiety disorders is the presence of autonomic inflexibility. As already mentioned, people who suffer from anxiety disorders chronically start higher on physiological measures of anxiety because of elevated sympathetic activity. In addition, these patients demonstrate less heart-rate variability in response to stressful stimuli, whereas nonanxious research subjects exhibit higher variable heart rates when exposed to stressors. A decrease in heart-rate variability has been correlated with increased cardiovascular morbidity (death). In addition, people with anxiety disorders take longer to have their heart rate return to baseline. It appears that the source of autonomic restriction is low PNS activity or tone. Studies comparing resting heart rates and heart-rate variability of children exhibiting behavioral inhibition (a precursor to social phobia and other anxiety disorders) with those of behaviorally uninhibited children replicate these findings. A pilot study has shown that cognitive-behavioral treatment seems to increase heart-rate variability and improve PNS tone.

### Asymmetrical Patterns of Brain Activity

Researchers have discovered that increased electrical activity, as measured by electroencephalogram (EEG), in the frontal or anterior right hemisphere seems to be correlated with increased negative affect and decreased positive affect. Increased EEG activity in the anterior left hemisphere is associated with heightened positive affect and decreased negative affect. These findings were first seen in patients with depression and then in patients with anxiety disorders. The hallmark of both of these emotional disorders is high experienced negative affect. Subjects with anxiety disorders showed this asymmetry both at rest and when confronted with anxiety-provoking stimuli, which indicates that this may be a biological marker for anxiety disorders.

The brain is divided into two hemispheres, with each hemisphere having a unique set of functions. The left side of the brain categorizes and organizes information, comprehends time, makes sequences, solves problems, and conducts analysis. This part of the brain recognizes and gives meaning to symbols (math and language) and modulates emotion by regulating the right hemisphere. The right hemisphere is the creative, nonverbal, emotional hemisphere. It recognizes faces, reads emotion, attaches emotional significance to events, sees spatial relationships, and listens for and creates rhythm and cadence in music, speech, and movement. It also facilitates emotional memory.

The hemispheric brain-wave asymmetry found in anxious subjects needs further exploration to determine its impact on the emotional and physiological experience of anxiety disorders. Early findings suggest its ability to differentiate anxious arousal (panic attack) from anxious apprehension (anticipatory worry), and it may also help distinguish anxiety disorders from depression.

### Identification of Specific Brain Structures Involved with Anxiety Disorders

In addition to our knowledge that the limbic system is involved in anxiety disorders, positron emission tomography (PET) has allowed scientists to observe more detailed activity, in particular, brain structures relative to anxiety. A radioactive isotope is attached to glucose (the main fuel of the brain) and is used to identify active parts of the brain when the patient is introduced to anxiety-provoking stimuli. On the PET scan, active areas literally light up and show researchers the specific anxiety-related areas. University of California, Los Angeles, researchers Lewis Baxter and Jeffrey Schwartz have discovered and examined a loop of electrical activity that travels from the frontal lobe—specifically the orbital frontal cortex (OFC), which is the underside of the frontal lobe—to the basal ganglia and back to the frontal lobe. This loop is an important anatomical structure implicated in OCD. The researchers have also been able to show a change in activity following cognitive-behavioral treatment, as well as drug treatment.

From the neuroimaging findings, Schwartz and other researchers propose that in the case of OCD, the basal-ganglia-determined activity of the OFC

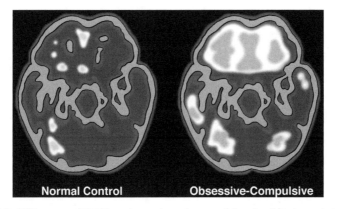

**Figure 5.2** PET scans of OCD patients show increased levels of brain activity in the orbital frontal cortex in comparison to controls. (Courtesy of Anil Shukla)

becomes locked to the activity of the basal ganglia. Thoughts become obsessive. Normally, the basal ganglia filter information, but in OCD this function is impaired. As a result, the error-detection activities of the OFC become overactive. Irrational fears become alarming and are believed to be true. This hyperactivity of the basal ganglia and OFC leads to thalamic dysfunction. Finally, the cingulate gyrus intensifies the feeling that something is wrong and creates the anxiety associated with irrational beliefs.

Evidence also exists that the basal ganglia are involved in social phobia. Altered dopamine function may decrease basal ganglia operation, which results in the impairment of normal social motor functions, such as eye movement, facial expressions, and speech. Researchers propose that this may lead to socially anxious thoughts and avoidance behavior.

Scientists theorize that an innate anxiety circuit exists that is related to the behavioral inhibition system, specifically the septohippocampal system. This system is a structure of fiber connections between the septum (a cortical structure) and the hippocampus of the limbic system and is influenced by the neurotransmitters norepinephrine and dopamine and the amygdala. This is the area that antianxiety medications affect. Research has also shown that various anxiety responses are handled by different aspects of the septohippocampal system, which also seems to be responsible for avoidance behavior. Much more research is needed to discover the finer workings of this system.

Another structural finding of interest is the discovery that the hippocampus is smaller in some patients with posttraumatic stress disorder. Researchers theorize that this may be the result of the degeneration of dendrites (see Figure 5.3a) within the hippocampus, which is likely caused by the increased presence of stress-released chemicals known as glucocorticoids, specifically cortisol.

Neuroimaging will be able to provide answers on brain changes such as this that occur following the experience of intense and chronic stress from anxiety disorders.

### The Neurochemical Role

Much of our initial understanding of neurochemical brain function in anxiety disorders grew out of the discovery of neurotransmitters and pharmaceutical research. In 1952, Betty Twarog, a recent doctoral graduate from Harvard, identified serotonin as a neurotransmitter and a year later, while working at the Cleveland Clinic, discovered its presence in the brain. Neurotransmitters are necessary for the transmission of electrical impulses from one nerve cell (neuron) to another. The impulse travels via neurotransmitters through the space between an axon of one neuron and a dendrite of another. The space is called the synapse.

In 1957, Swedish researcher Arvid Carlsson identified another neurotransmitter, known as dopamine. The early research on these neurotransmitters was done in the hope of finding the causes of schizophrenia and other psychotic disorders, but it soon became apparent that the neurotransmitters were also implicated in depression.

Research on psychotic disorders that had produced the discoveries of serotonin and dopamine became very useful in the development of antidepressants. It was hypothesized that serotonin worked on the PNS to calm the organism. Deficiencies in serotonin and dopamine were observed concurrently with depression. The early antidepressants (monamine oxidase inhibitors) were found to boost the availability of these neurotransmitters and to reduce depressive symptoms in some people. Since this was found to also reduce anxiety, the research on these neurotransmitters shed light on the chemical workings of anxiety as well.

As the effects of the tricyclic antidepressants were examined, further discoveries were made about the specific mechanism involved in increasing available serotonin and dopamine. The tricyclics prevented the neurons from reabsorbing serotonin after it had been released into the synapse, thus illuminating the reuptake mechanism in neurons. Recent research indicates that selective serotonin reuptake inhibitors may also stimulate the growth of serotonin-specific neurons, which would increase the number of neurons available to utilize serotonin.

It was believed that another neurotransmitter, norepinephrine (also called noradrenaline), alerts and brings the organism to the fight-or-flight mode. Studies conducted in the late 1970s and early 1980s further highlighted the

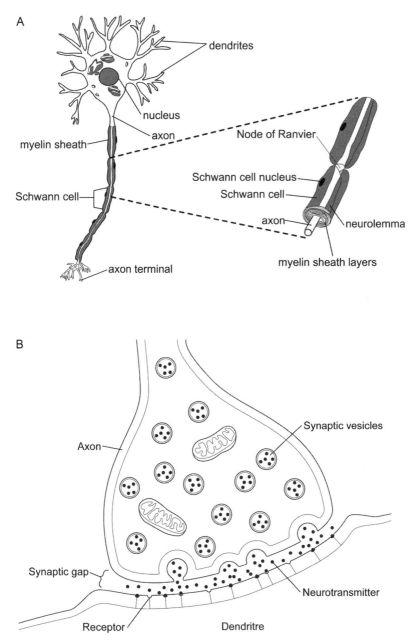

**Figure 5.3** a, Anatomy of the neuron. b, Neurotransmission. (Courtesy of Jeff Dixon)

role of the noradrenergic system (source of noradrenaline or norepinephrine) and its major center, the locus ceruleus. Norepinephrine is produced and regulated by the locus ceruleus and other nuclei in the brain stem. The locus ceruleus is connected to the cerebral cortex and the limbic system, as well as other brain structures. Stimulation of the locus ceruleus increases the available norepinephrine and induces anxiety and panic through activation of the ANS.

Research on the effects of benzodiazepines also reveals some interesting discoveries. Receptor sites for benzodiazepines were discovered, which leads to the conclusion that there are naturally occurring anxiety-reducing chemicals that bind to the same receptor sites. In addition, it was observed that the inhibitory neurotransmitter GABA facilitates the binding of benzodiazepines to their receptors. This amino acid is believed to induce relaxation and has become available as a dietary supplement. This supplement is a naturopathic remedy that is sold without the necessary randomized and controlled double-blind studies and therefore lacks Food and Drug Administration approval.

The so-called benzodiazepine-GABA system apparently plays a role in the experience of generalized anxiety disorder (GAD). It appears that sufferers of GAD have fewer benzodiazepine receptors, as do people who suffer from chronic stress. The hormone cortisol (see Figure 5.5) is released during the

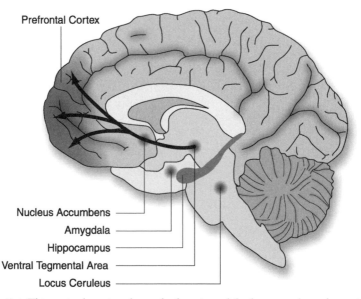

**Figure 5.4** This sagittal section shows the location of the locus ceruleus, the main center of the noradrenergic system, alongside the primary structures of the mesolimbic dopamine pathway. (Courtesy of Kathryn H. Hollen)

experience of stress. When a person is chronically anxious or under stress, high levels of cortisol reduce the number of available benzodiazepine receptor sites. The administration of an effective benzodiazepine increases the number of these receptor sites. Unfortunately, the long-term use of benzodiazepines is problematic because of potential addiction. Gabapentin is a chemical analogue (a chemical with a similar molecular structure) of GABA that is used as an antiseizure medicine; it has shown promise in the treatment of GAD. The search for the body's own naturally occurring anxiolytic substances continues.

The hypothalamic-pituitary-adrenal (HPA) axis plays a major role in the reaction to stress and therefore in the symptomatology of anxiety disorders. The HPA axis is a complex system of influences and feedback loops that regulate the stress response and certain bodily functions. Stressors stimulate the limbic system, the locus ceruleus, and the cerebral cortex, which in turn activate corticotropin-releasing hormone (CRH), which is stored predominantly in the hypothalamus and amygdala. CRH and related hormones stimulate the pituitary and adrenal glands to release adrenocorticotropic hormone (ACTH), which in turn produces and releases cortisol, which has an impact on the ANS. It has also been discovered that CRH also influences other brain and behavioral reactions. Recent findings indicate that CRH release is also affected by the benzodiazepine-GABA system, as well as serotonin, dopamine, and norepinephrine. It has been observed that elevated levels of CRH in the

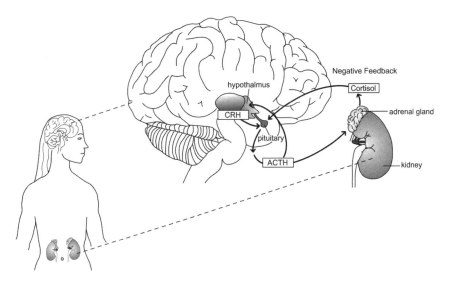

**Figure 5.5** The hypothalamic-pituitary-adrenal axis is a complex system that regulates the stress response and certain bodily functions.

locus ceruleus induce anxious behavior in animals. Studies on CRH and the HPA axis, which is responsible for the production and mediation of CRH, are helping scientists understand the integration of all these systems that underpin anxiety disorders.

As mentioned, cortisol is a hormone that is released by the adrenal gland when the HPA axis and SNS are activated to assist in the fight-or-flight response. Feedback to the HPA axis decreases the release of CRH, ACTH, and therefore levels of cortisol. Research has shown that early life exposure to predictable and controllable stressful situations helps a person develop resilience, or good stress tolerance, and leads to minimal cortisol production. On the other hand, the early experience of unpredictable and uncontrollable stressors, as in the case of child abuse, chronically increases cortisol levels. The body and brain are affected in negative ways when cortisol levels remain high.

## THE ROLE OF EXPERIENCE AND LEARNING (PSYCHOLOGY) IN BRAIN FUNCTION

In the latter part of the twentieth century, animal research began to indicate that experience and learning had an effect on brain structure and functioning. The prior acquisition of coping skills mediated neurotransmitter activity when an animal was exposed to later stressors. Other researchers observed differences in the number of receptor sites and sensitivity of synapses (synaptic strength) based on prior learning and conditioning. Eric Kandel was awarded the Nobel Prize in Physiology in 2000 (along with Carlsson and Paul Greengard) for his work on the relationship of learning and brain function. He was able to show that fear conditioning results in permanent increases in receptors and neurotransmitters. Kandel proposed that learning activates specific genes related to the vulnerability to anxiety disorders, which leads to changes in brain structure and functioning. These changes are undone if the behavior (for example, avoidance) is extinguished. Studies conducted following Kandel's early work have supported his findings, giving credibility to the stress-diathesis model, which states that the genetic predisposition for an anxiety disorder is present and is activated by life experiences and learning. The other interesting finding is the reversibility of these neural changes following corrective interventions or treatment. This has been further confirmed by the posttreatment testing of neurotransmitter levels and neuroimaging studies (such as Schwartz and Baxter's work with OCD).

Animal and human studies of the impact of early stressful experiences on later behaviors and the etiology of anxiety disorders are indicating that chronic changes occur in the development of brain structures and functioning. It seems evident that the development of the HPA axis is affected, resulting in increased levels of CRH and increased reactivity that persists into adult life.

The phenomenon of uncued (out-of-the-blue) panic attacks, which are intense bursts of fight-or-flight response from the ANS, are experienced by a large percentage of the population. For many people, this "false alarm" experience never becomes panic disorder. It appears that a psychological and biological predisposition plus life stress contributes to the occurrence of false alarms. Those who develop panic disorder appear to have the chronic hyperarousal associated with anxiety disorders. In addition, it is likely that for panic patients, learning plays a significant role in the development of the disorder. False alarms become conditioned alarms, likely increasing anxiety-related receptor and neurotransmitter levels as the learning is strengthened. Early experiences, such as separation and its resulting anxiety, may lead to learning that the bodily sensations associated with fear are aversive and dangerous. Consequently, anxiety sensitivity develops, and following an initial false alarm, the person learns to fear the panic attacks, thereby increasing the conditioning and the likelihood of subsequent attacks. Scientists have been unable to find distinctive underlying biological processes for panic disorder, but there seems to be some neurological distinction between those who develop panic disorder, those who have false alarms and never develop panic disorder, and those with GAD.

## THE PHYSICAL EFFECTS OF ANXIETY

As mentioned earlier, increased and chronic levels of cortisol have a negative impact on the body and the immune system. Cortisol's function is to bring the body to a state that will enhance its response to stress. It raises blood pressure, increases glucose production for energy, and produces a variety of other changes in service to the SNS response. Unfortunately, long-term exposure to cortisol is detrimental to the body. It causes a persistent rise in blood pressure, which increases the likelihood of heart attack and stroke. In addition, cortisol can create hyperglycemia (high blood sugar), which can lead to diabetes. Cortisol affects the absorption of calcium and therefore decreases bone formation. This can lead to osteoporosis, a disease in which decreased bone density leads to fragility of the bones and increased breakage. Cortisol also reduces the size of the hippocampus in patients with posttraumatic stress disorder. The damage of hippocampal cells results in impaired learning and therefore impaired cognitive functioning. High, sustained levels of cortisol reduce the effectiveness of the immune system, which can lead to any number of illnesses and delay healing. In recent years, it has been discovered that high cortisol levels increase weight gain and the storing of fat around the abdomen.

Chronically high levels of cortisol cause fatigue, gastrointestinal problems, and premature aging. The wear and tear on the body caused by hyperreactivity and chronic stress is a significant reason to encourage early treatment of anxiety disorders. Research has also indicated that overactivity of the HPA axis is correlated with depression. This makes sense, given that depression and anxiety disorders frequently co-occur, with the depression often developing subsequent to the anxiety disorder.

Additional ailments are tied to anxiety disorders, including irritable bowel syndrome, migraine headaches, insomnia, and muscle aches. It is believed that autoimmune illnesses, such as rheumatoid arthritis, are aggravated by the high levels of ANS activity common to most anxiety disorders. Scientists have theorized that some cancers are also related to high stress levels. Ongoing research is exploring this premise.

## A FINAL NOTE

The discovery of neurotransmitters and the emerging knowledge of the function of specific brain structures in the early twentieth century have produced a much more complex and sophisticated understanding of the biological workings of anxiety disorders. Rapidly advancing technologies are allowing us to look forward to even greater knowledge and understanding as research progresses. As we further comprehend how these disorders work at the psycho-neurobiological level, we will be able to develop more effective treatment and preventive strategies.

# 6

# Assessment and Diagnosis

 arissa flopped into a chair in the college student union lounge. She was exhausted. Arriving only three weeks earlier to begin her freshman year at the university, she had had a rough time. Her summer had been a whirlwind of activity, and although she had felt somewhat nervous, Marissa was mostly excited and looking forward to this new phase of her life. That was why she just couldn't understand what was happening to her.

On her third day of classes, Marissa had walked into her chemistry lecture and felt slightly nauseated and also noticed that her heart was racing. Instantly, she was overwhelmed by feelings of dread and panic. Fearing that her classmates would notice her intense anxiety, Marissa fled the room. These attacks continued over the next few weeks, and although she was miserable, she toughed it out. Soon Marissa dreaded chemistry and, on occasion, felt her anxiety build before she entered the classroom. Her life became punctuated by periods of overwhelming anxiety. Distracted in class, she was falling behind and becoming increasingly exhausted.

As she sat in the student union, Marissa realized she could not continue to live this way. She considered going home, dropping out and attending community college, taking a year off, or just forgetting about the whole college thing altogether. Her parents were unaware of what was going on with her anxiety; she was too embarrassed to tell them, thinking she was just weak-willed and not up to the challenge of being away from home. Marissa had talked to the resident adviser (RA) in her dorm, who suggested that she consult someone at the student counseling center. At least the RA had been understanding and didn't just give her a pep talk, which was what she had feared.

"Okay," she said to herself, "I just have to bite the bullet and do this." She walked to the counseling center, drew a deep breath and opened the door. The receptionist greeted her and asked her to fill out an intake form. In addition to her name, address, and phone number, this form allowed space for her to describe what was troubling her. Marissa then met briefly with a counselor who asked her some questions, including how soon she felt she needed to see someone and whether she felt at risk for hurting herself. Marissa said she felt safe and that she could wait a day or two, but no more. An appointment was set for the next day for an assessment that would begin her treatment. For the first time since she had the initial panic attack, Marissa felt hopeful.

## ASSESSMENT

The first step in treatment is always a thorough assessment. The presenting problem is the patient's sense of what is most troubling. Developing a complete picture of the presenting problem is crucial because it is often the primary diagnosis. It is also important to discover any comorbid diagnoses and complicating issues. Complicating factors include physical illnesses, environmental stressors, and other life circumstances. In addition, the clinician should evaluate patient strengths and resources, such as intelligence, insight, motivation, and supports. Much of this information is gathered by the clinician in an interview format. In addition, the therapist may use assessment tools, which are either structured interviews administered by the clinician or questionnaires completed by either the patient or the clinician.

Mental health issues are not as easily diagnosed as clearly observable physical maladies. A broken bone is diagnosed on the basis of x-ray results. The mental health clinician relies on patient report, his or her own observations, and reports by family members, if available. Assessment tools are valuable, as they are researched and tested for reliability (the ability to measure the same phenomena repeatedly) and validity (the ability to measure the construct in question, such as social anxiety).

An excellent assessment tool for anxiety disorders is the *Anxiety Disorders Interview Schedule IV* (*ADIS-IV*) and its lifetime version. These are structured interviews that include the *DSM-IV* criteria for all the anxiety, mood, and substance abuse/dependence disorders. An example of the initial questions from the *ADIS-IV* for panic disorder follows:

1a. Do you currently have times when you feel a sudden rush of intense fear or discomfort?

_____Yes _____No

If YES, skip to 2a.

b. If NO, Have you <u>ever</u> had times when you have felt a sudden rush of intense fear or discomfort?

_____Yes _____No

If YES, When was the most recent time this occurred?

_____

\*\*\*\*\*\*\*\*\*\*\*\*\*\*\*\*\*\*\*\*\*\*\*\*\*\*\*\*\*\*\*\*\*\*\*\*\*\*\*\*\*\*\*\*\*\*\*\*\*\*\*\*\*\*\*\*\*\*\*\*\*\*\*\*

If YES to either 1a. or 1b., or uncertain, continue inquiry.
Otherwise skip to AGORAPHOBIA (p. 8)

\*\*\*\*\*\*\*\*\*\*\*\*\*\*\*\*\*\*\*\*\*\*\*\*\*\*\*\*\*\*\*\*\*\*\*\*\*\*\*\*\*\*\*\*\*\*\*\*\*\*\*\*\*\*\*\*\*\*\*\*\*\*\*\*

(Brown, DiNardo, and Barlow, p. 3)

The *ADIS-IV* is constructed so that the essential conditions for a disorder are asked first. If the conditions are met, the interviewer proceeds through the questions soliciting information about the details of the disorder; however, if they are not met, the interviewer moves on to the next disorder. This instrument also yields ratings for the severity and impairment levels of the disorders. The *ADIS-IV* allows for the collection of demographic data, life stressors, and life conditions. It should be rounded out by clinician questioning on any additional information the clinician deems essential, such as family history.

The *ADIS-IV* is a well-regarded and validated instrument that is useful for both clinical and research purposes. In addition, there is a plethora of tools to assess and rate anxiety disorders, many of which were generated for use in research. Discussion here will focus on clinical practice and some of the instruments that have proven applicability in that setting.

Excellent assessment tools currently allow for the establishment of a baseline (how the patient is doing prior to treatment) and the measurement of progress. The Burns Anxiety Inventory is a rating scale of worry thoughts, anxiety experience, and physical symptoms. The Fear and Avoidance Hierarchy is an excellent tool for assessing symptomatology and evaluating progress in patients with panic disorder. The patient and clinician together list the activities that are problematic. The patient then gives a rating (0–10) of the level of anxiety and avoidance of each feared situation.

Since many patients with an anxiety disorder also suffer from depression, it is wise to evaluate depression at the commencement of treatment and periodically as treatment progresses. The Beck Depression Inventory II (BDI) is a well-respected and easily completed assessment of depressive affect that many clinicians use to monitor mood regardless of the primary diagnosis. The BDI is a twenty-one-item questionnaire that the patient can complete in a matter of minutes. It measures the severity of depressive mood by asking patients to rate their experience of the common symptoms of depression in the following manner:

1. Sadness

    ° I do not feel sad.
    ° I feel sad much of the time.
    ° I am sad all the time.
    ° I am so sad and unhappy that I can't stand it.

Instruments that elicit information about specific symptoms are particularly useful beyond the *ADIS-IV* for disorders such as obsessive-compulsive disorder (OCD) and posttraumatic stress disorder (PTSD). The Yale-Brown Obsessive-Compulsive Scale (Y-BOCS) is a checklist of obsessions and compulsions and a series of rating scales for severity and impairment. It is used to develop a hierarchy of symptoms in preparation for treatment and can later be used to evaluate progress. Although there are many scales and structured interviews for PTSD with excellent reliability and validity, many are best suited for research. A good clinical and research scale is the PTSD Symptom Scale-Interview, which lists the seventeen criteria of the PTSD diagnosis and allows for rating of the severity of the symptoms.

Although clinicians have a variety of tools available to assist in assessment, they must never forget the importance of the clinical interview and the ongoing assessment that each session yields. In addition to providing information for diagnosis, the clinician also has a wealth of data with that to conduct treatment.

Patients presenting with anxiety disorders need to be assessed carefully for comorbidity because anxiety disorders are associated with numerous illnesses, such as gastrointestinal difficulties, hypertension, pulmonary disorders, cardiac disorders, genitourinary problems, and migraine headaches, as well as other mental disorders.

When possible, and always with the patient's permission, the clinician can also gather information from collateral sources. If a family member accompanies the patient to the assessment, he or she can offer a perspective on behavior of which the patient may not be aware or about which the patient may tend to hold back. Summaries from prior treatment or psychological testing should be obtained when possible, and collaboration should occur with any current or referring treatment providers.

## The Clinical Interview

The clinical interview includes gathering information on the presenting problem and its history; other complaints, sleep and eating patterns; drug, tobacco, and alcohol use; brief medical history, treatment, and current medications; nutrition and exercise patterns; psychological/psychiatric treatment history, suicidal ideation and suicide attempt history; family composition; life circumstances, including financial, educational, and job status, religious involvement, and supports (friends, self-help groups, etc.); and a mental status exam.

### The Psychiatric Mental Status Exam (MSE)

I.  Appearance and behavior
    Dress, grooming, hygiene
    Posture
    Gait and motor coordination and activity
    Other mannerisms or behaviors

II. Manner and approach
    Interpersonal characteristics and approach to evaluation
    Speech
        Rate
        Quantity
        Volume (loudness)
        Fluency
        Clarity (articulation)
    Eye contact
    Expressive language
    Receptive language

III. Mood and affect
    Mood: pervasive and maintained emotional state
    Affect: current outward manifestation of mood
    Intensity
    Lability (changeability of mood)
    Appropriateness
    Rapport
    Facial and emotional expressions

*(Continued)*

Suicidal and homicidal ideation
Risk for violence

IV. Orientation, alertness, and thought processes
Orientation (person, place, time)
Alertness
Coherence
Concentration and attention
Thought processes
Recall and memory
Hallucinations and delusions

There are excellent sources for MSE formatting and questions, including the Mini-Mental Status Exam (Folstein et al. 1975).

---

## DIAGNOSIS OF THE SPECIFIC ANXIETY DISORDERS

Since researchers, clinicians, and patients need a common language for accurate communication, the history of mental illness and anxiety disorders shows an ever-evolving attempt to classify and categorize the phenomena of anxiety. Some clinicians and mental health advocacy groups have taken issue with this effort over the years, shying away from the idea of attaching labels to patients. Nevertheless, the consensus is that these categories and criteria—as imperfect as they are—are extremely beneficial when designing treatment plans for patients and communicating with other health professionals. In addition, for research to have any validity and reliability, it is essential that scientists agree upon what phenomena they are investigating. Diagnostic categories and their criteria are fluid, as we continue to learn more about the disorders and their presentation, course, accompanying features, and distinction from other disorders.

The *Diagnostic and Statistical Manual* (DSM) series has now been updated five times since its inception in 1952. Controversial categories, such as the old diagnosis of homosexuality, have been dropped. The first two editions were psychodynamically based, but a major shift occurred with the publication of *DSM-III* in 1980. Beginning with *DSM-III*, the classification has had more of a medical orientation and is atheoretical regarding etiology of disorders. In the latest revision, the *DSM-IV Text Revision* (*DSM-IV-TR*), there was no change made to diagnostic criteria; however, further supporting evidence and updated statistics were added to the text. The next version, *DSM-V*, is currently under development and is a collaborative effort that involves the publisher (the

American Psychiatric Association) and the U.S. National Institutes of Health, specifically the National Institute on Alcohol Abuse and Alcoholism, the National Institute on Drug Abuse, and the National Institute of Mental Health. Because the goal is to make the *DSM* globally relevant, its collaborators include representatives from the World Health Organization and the World Psychiatric Association.

The *DSM-IV-TR* criteria for each anxiety disorder are described in the following section. In addition, specific cases are presented to give the reader a more direct feel for the disorders. In the *DSM*, the disorders are identified by name and a numeric code. The numeric code is consistent with the codes of the *International Statistical Classification of Diseases and Related Health Problems-Tenth Version (ICD-10)*, which is the accepted global classification of medical diseases. The *DSM* provides a variety of information about each disorder, including epidemiology; cultural and gender factors; course of the illness; qualifiers, such as the subtype of specific phobia; and associated features, such as the presence of perfectionism with OCD. The *DSM* also informs the reader about common comorbid conditions. Differential criteria are also presented that include possible rule-outs (e.g., the disturbance is not due to the direct physiological effects of a substance) and possible alternative diagnoses (e.g., the anxiety and the particular symptoms are not better accounted for by another mental disorder). Often contingencies must be met in terms of the length of time of the disturbance, the number of symptoms out of the full criteria that must be met to meet the diagnosis, age of onset, and interference in functioning. For all the disorders except generalized anxiety disorder (GAD), the symptom criteria are presented here, and the rule-outs and associated features are excluded. The full criteria for GAD are presented in order to demonstrate the aforementioned contingencies. The reader can refer to the *DSM* for full information on each disorder.

### Diagnostic Criteria for Generalized Anxiety Disorder (300.02)

Reprinted with permission from the *Diagnostic and Statistical Manual of Mental Disorders, Fourth Edition, Text Revision* (2000), American Psychiatric Association.

A. Excessive anxiety and worry (apprehensive expectation), occurring more days than not for at least 6 months, about a number of events or activities (such as work or school performance).
B. The person finds it difficult to control the worry.

C. The anxiety and worry are associated with three (or more) of the following six symptoms (with at least some symptoms present for more days than not for the past 6 months). Note: Only one item is required in children.
   (1) restlessness or feeling keyed up or on edge
   (2) being easily fatigued
   (3) difficulty concentrating or mind going blank
   (4) irritability
   (5) muscle tension
   (6) sleep disturbance (difficulty falling or staying asleep, or restless unsatisfying sleep)

D. The focus of the anxiety and worry is not confined to features of an Axis I disorder, e.g., the anxiety or worry is not about having a Panic Attack (as in Panic Disorder), being embarrassed in public (as in Social Phobia), being contaminated (as in Obsessive-Compulsive Disorder), being away from home or close relatives (as in Separation Anxiety Disorder), gaining weight (as in Anorexia Nervosa), having multiple physical complaints (as in Somatization Disorder), or having a serious illness (as in Hypochondriasis), and the anxiety and worry do not occur exclusively during Posttraumatic Stress Disorder.

E. The anxiety, worry, or physical symptoms cause clinically significant distress or impairment in social, occupational, or other important areas of functioning.

F. The disturbance is not due to the direct physiological effects of a substance (e.g., a drug of abuse, a medication) or a general medical condition (e.g., hyperthyroidism) and does not occur exclusively during a Mood Disorder, a Psychotic Disorder, or a Pervasive Developmental Disorder.

### Aubrey's Story

Aubrey had always been what her mother described as "a nervous kid" who worried about all aspects of her life and needed constant reassurance when confronting new situations. When "obsessing" or ruminating about anxiety-provoking situations, she would have trouble sleeping, become irritable, have difficulty concentrating, lose her appetite, get diarrhea, and lose weight. The intensification in Aubrey's anxiety after her first child was born prompted her to come in for therapy. Her anxiety encompassed everything from world events to the well-being of her family. Aubrey found herself focusing on any indications she believed to be signs of poor health in herself and her infant. Unlike a person with hypochondriasis, she was able to be reassured about each occurrence, but she would then find something else to worry about. Her husband had grown weary of her nervousness, reassurance seeking, and consequent irritability and encouraged her to seek treatment when her symptoms intensified. Aubrey desperately wanted to feel relaxed with her new baby and did not want to impart her anxiety to her son.

### Diagnostic Criteria for Specific Phobia (300.29)

Specific phobias are characterized by a dramatic and persistent fear of an object or situation that is unreasonable and excessive. Examples of specific phobias include flying, heights, animals, receiving an injection, and seeing blood. Exposure to the situation or object always elicits an immediate panic-like attack. The person is aware that the response is excessive or unreasonable and may avoid the situation whenever possible. The avoidance, anxious apprehension, or distress interferes with the person's functioning (normal routine, occupation, social activities, or relationships).

#### A Fear of Heights

Bob was thirty-two years old when he came in for treatment for a phobia of heights. Although he was successful in his career, Bob described himself as a relatively anxious person who startled easily and was prone to worry about the quality of his work and his health. His childhood had been stressful, since his sister had suffered from a severe developmental disability. Bob could not recall a precipitating event for his fear of heights but did report that he had been uncomfortable with heights for as long as he could remember. What prompted his request for treatment was that he now worked in a building with a multi-story atrium in the center that he could not avoid. Bob dreaded going to work and, while at work, dreaded leaving his suite to go to lunch or the restroom.

### Diagnostic Criteria for Obsessive-Compulsive Disorder (300.3)

Obsessive-compulsive disorder is characterized by the presence of either obsessions or compulsions. Obsessions are recurrent or persistent thoughts, images, or impulses that are intrusive and cause marked anxiety or distress which the person tries to suppress or neutralize. The obsessions are not excessive worry about real-life problems, and the person is aware that they are a product of his or her own mind. Compulsions are repetitive behaviors or thoughts which are intended to provide relief from the distress of the obsessions or to prevent a feared event. The compulsions are excessive and are not connected in a realistic way to what they are designed to neutralize or prevent (such as tapping the wall to prevent overhead planes from crashing). Compulsions include such behaviors as hand washing, checking, praying, or counting and consume at least one hour per day. The distress and interference impedes functioning. Generally the person recognizes that the obsessions or compulsions are excessive or unreasonable (this does not apply to children). The clinician must specify if the patient cannot adequately assess his condition.

### The Terror of Contamination

Robin was a forty-seven-year-old writer and full-time mother of two children who came into therapy after years of only receiving medication treatment (Luvox) for her condition. She wanted to try the cognitive-behavioral approach of "exposure and response prevention" because the medication was only mildly helpful and she disliked the side effects. Robin's obsessions were focused on the fear that she or her children would contract HIV through casual contact with an infected person's blood. She refused to eat in restaurants, and grocery shopping became a time-consuming and laborious ordeal. Robin would check each item for any signs of blood and would use wipes to clean her hands if "blood" was detected. She had a hard time distinguishing the source of red or brown marks, so she always erred on the side of caution. She would secretly scrutinize the check-out clerks to ensure that they had no cuts on their hands. When Robin got home with her groceries, she would wash the packaging and throw out any items that she thought were contaminated.

Workers in the house were particularly distressing to Robin, and she would compulsively scrub everything they had touched. Even after scrubbing (doorknobs, walls, appliances, toilets), she could not bring herself to touch the items for many months. Robin wore gloves to open the mail and would send back anything with a red or brown smudge on the packaging. Her hands were raw and cracked from the excessive washing. Going to the doctor was extremely difficult for her, as she believed that a doctor's office was most certainly contaminated. She would scrutinize the nurse and physician for hand washing and new glove use, and she would shower and launder her clothes upon returning home. Exhausted and tormented, Robin complained that she was paralyzed by her fears and had no time to pursue her writing or to be an involved parent and wife. The OCD was totally consuming her life. She had many days when she felt depressed and discouraged. Robin knew that at some level, her concerns were unreasonable, yet she marveled that other people were so blasé about the potential for HIV contamination. Her husband had become increasingly annoyed with her symptoms, and she was concerned about the effect that she was having on her children, who were now old enough to be aware of her behavior.

## A Family Illness

After Robin was in treatment for three years, she asked whether her son could also be evaluated for OCD. Josh was fourteen years old and in the ninth grade. He was an excellent student and active in sports. He had confided in his mother that he found himself spending a large amount of time worrying about his academic standing and became increasingly perfectionistic about his performance in school. Josh started to reread and rewrite, never feeling that his work was good enough. He also found himself avoiding developmentally delayed students because of his fear that proximity to them would affect his brain and make him lose his intelligence.

## Diagnostic Criteria for Panic Disorder with Agoraphobia (300.21), without Agoraphobia (300.01), and Agoraphobia without a History of Panic Disorder (300.22)

Panic disorder is defined by the presence of recurrent and, initially, unexpected panic attacks, at least one of which has been followed by at least one month of persistent worry about having additional attacks and the consequences such as losing control, having a heart attack, or "going crazy." The person also has a significant change in behavior related to the attacks. The presence of agoraphobia is marked by either avoiding situations outside the home or enduring these situations with dread.

A panic attack is characterized by at least four of the following symptoms: tachycardia (rapid heart beat), shortness of breath or smothering sensations, flushing or chills, trembling or shaking, tingling sensations in the extremities, nausea or queasy stomach, feeling of choking, derealization (an altered sense of reality) or depersonalization (being detached from oneself), sweating, chest pain or discomfort, and fear of going crazy or dying. A limited panic attack is defined by the presence of no more than four of these symptoms.

## The Specter of Panic

A twenty-nine-year-old chief medical resident at a renowned teaching hospital, Laura had exhibited the ability to think quickly and make good decisions. During a grand rounds meeting, an older physician who was known for his abrupt and harsh style fired questions at her. Unexpectedly, Laura had a panic attack. She felt a sudden rush of heat, her heart began to race, and she flushed and broke into a sweat, began to tremble, and totally lost her concentration and ability to speak. She struggled to finish her presentation and quickly left the room. Once out of the situation, Laura began to calm down, but she was very embarrassed and felt horribly drained. The specter of this event haunted her, and when the next staff meeting approached, she found herself dreading the gathering. She became so anxious that she was nauseated and endured the meeting with building terror. The following week, Laura went to the staff meeting in a very high state of anxious arousal. She did her presentation with a wavering voice but got through it. At this point, she called to make an appointment for therapy. By the time she came in for the appointment two weeks later, her anxious apprehension had generalized to other situations. Laura became fearful of leading resident meetings, doing daily rounds, and even getting together with a group of her friends. She was exhausted and felt that the panic was an ever-present threat.

Laura revealed that numerous people in her family, including her mother and grandmother, suffered from GAD. To her knowledge, no one else in her family suffered from panic disorder. Laura herself had always been slightly anxious and a bit of a worrier, but never to the point of meeting the diagnostic criteria for an anxiety disorder.

### Diagnostic Criteria for Acute Stress Disorder (308.3)

The person with acute stress disorder (or posttraumatic stress disorder) has been exposed to a traumatic event in which he or she experienced, witnessed, or was confronted with an event(s) that involved actual or threatened death or serious injury, or a threat to the physical integrity of self or others. The response involved intense fear, helplessness, or horror. Either during or after the event, the person has at least three of the following dissociative symptoms: a sense of numbing, detachment or estrangement from others, an absence of emotional responsiveness, a reduction in awareness of his or her surroundings (e.g., "being in a daze"), derealization, depersonalization, and dissociative amnesia (inability to recall an important aspect of the trauma). Additionally, the traumatic event is persistently reexperienced in at least one of the following ways: recurrent images, thoughts, dreams, illusions, flashback episodes (a sense of reliving the experience) or distress on exposure to reminders of the traumatic event. The patient avoids any stimuli which arouse recollections of the trauma including thoughts, feelings, conversations, activities, places, and people. The person has significantly increased anxious arousal manifested in difficulty sleeping, irritability, poor concentration, hypervigilance, exaggerated startle response, and motor restlessness. There is impairment in functioning. Acute stress disorder lasts for at least two days, no more than four weeks, and begins within one month of the traumatic event.

### Diagnostic Criteria for Posttraumatic Stress Disorder (309.81)

Posttraumatic stress disorder (PTSD) is characterized by the same symptoms as acute stress disorder; however, the duration of the disorder must be over one month. An acute PTSD versus chronic PTSD specification is made for less than three months in length versus more than three months, respectively. Also "late onset" is designated if the onset is six months after the occurrence of the event. In addition to the aforementioned symptoms, PTSD can also include a sense of a foreshortened future whereby the person does not expect to have a career, marriage, children, or a normal life span.

### A Psychological Casualty of War

John was in his second tour of duty in Iraq and was assigned to a ground unit responsible for civilian security in an urban area. He was present when suicide bombers in a truck attacked a local police barracks, resulting in the death and dismemberment of numerous Iraqi police officers and American troops. John was not physically injured, and he returned to duty following the event. Immediately following the event, he noticed that he was hyperalert to vehicles with an engine sound similar to that of the truck involved in the bombing. John returned home several months later following the completion of his tour. Once home, his sleep became disrupted, as he would awaken to any loud sound in the night. His dreams began to be focused on the traumatic event and its gruesome details. John felt numb much of the time and was irritated by his children's and wife's presence and demands. He spent more and more time out of the house at a local pub and returned home intoxicated. John would not talk about his Iraq duty and refused to see a friend who had been in his battalion. Job seeking was an overwhelming task for him. His wife shared her concerns with him and he agreed to go to the local office of Veterans Affairs for an evaluation. Although John had not suffered from an anxiety disorder before experiencing these symptoms, he did have a family history of GAD and depression.

### Diagnostic Criteria for Social Phobia (300.23)

Social phobia or social anxiety is the fear of being negatively evaluated, embarrassed, or humiliated in social situations. Experiencing or anticipating the feared situation provokes an anxiety response, which may take the form of a situationally-bound panic attack. The person either avoids such situations or endures them with dread. The sufferer of social phobia is aware that the response is excessive and unreasonable. In children, the anxiety may be expressed by crying, tantrums, freezing, or shrinking from social situations with unfamiliar people. Children are often not aware that their response is excessive.

### The Fear of Embarrassment

Amanda was described by her mother as a shy, reserved child who had suffered from separation anxiety. In school, she did not easily relate to other children and was reluctant to participate in class. She presented for treatment at the age of twenty-one after completing college. Amanda had been able to establish some friendships, but she had difficulty meeting new people, being assertive and was extremely uncomfortable eating in front of others. Amanda had decided to come to therapy because she was having significant anxiety about interviewing for jobs.

## Substance-Induced Anxiety Disorder and Anxiety Disorder due to . . . [Indicate the General Medical Condition] (293.84)

Two diagnostic categories are used to designate anxiety syndromes that are produced by either substances or a physical illness. Significant anxiety, panic attacks, obsessions, or compulsions may be experienced with either of these circumstances. The diagnoses are based on history and a co-occurring substance use or physical illness. Neither diagnosis would be made if there were a pre-existing anxiety disorder. The substance-induced anxiety disorders are coded with the substance-specific identifiers from the substance-related disorders section of the DSM. Additionally, the side effects of some medications include anxiety symptoms.

A variety of physical changes or illnesses can induce the symptoms of anxiety. Studies have shown that anxiety can be triggered by hyperthyroidism, hypothyroidism, pneumonia, arteriosclerotic vascular disease, ulcerative colitis, and hypochromic anemia. Additionally, endocrine alterations, such as menopause or insufficient testosterone, can provoke anxiety symptoms.

## Anxiety Disorder Not Otherwise Specified (NOS) (300.00)

This category includes disorders with significant anxiety or phobic avoidance that do not meet the criteria for any of the specific anxiety disorders or other mental disorder in which anxiety is a component (e.g., adjustment disorder with anxiety). An example of this would be a situation in which the patient experiences mixed depressive affect and anxiety, but does not meet criteria for a mood or anxiety disorder.

## SUMMARY

Clinicians, once informed by clinical interview, assessment instruments, any collateral data, and their clinical impressions, can arrive at a diagnostic framework and begin to formulate a treatment plan in collaboration with the patient. Severity and level of impairment lead to a recommendation about level of care and the need for a medication trial or change. The patient and clinician or treatment team (if at a higher level of care) will set goals and objectives for treatment based on the data gathered and the diagnosis, which is why the initial assessment period is so important.

After her first meeting with Marissa, the counselor was able to assess that Marissa was most likely suffering from panic attacks. Marissa had had a complete physical before beginning college, which had eliminated any physical causes for her attacks. The counselor began to administer the *ADIS-IV* to get a complete picture of the symptoms that Marissa was experiencing and to determine whether she was also suffering from another anxiety or mood disorder. The counselor provided Marissa with information about panic disorder and panic attacks and was able to explain how treatment would proceed. Armed with new knowledge and a course of action, Marissa felt great relief. The following week, she attended her second session, in which the counselor completed the *ADIS-IV* and further evaluated whether Marissa would benefit from medication as well as therapy.

# 7

# Treatment of Anxiety Disorders

Marissa's second session proceeded with the completion of the formal assessment. Her psychologist, Dr. Hamilton, thought that Marissa would benefit from medication to help her cope better. This was suggested particularly in light of the fact that the semester was moving forward and that she was already overwhelmed. Dr. Hamilton referred her to see the counseling center psychiatrist, Dr. Neville. Dr. Neville concurred and prescribed Zoloft, a selective serotonin reuptake inhibitor (SSRI) and Ativan, a benzodiazepine. The plan was to gradually increase the Zoloft, which would take up to six weeks to be effective, and to use the Ativan to bring relief now. Eventually the Ativan would be discontinued, especially after Marissa was able to use cognitive-behavioral strategies to manage her panic attacks.

Dr. Hamilton taught Marissa how panic attacks happen and how our thoughts can make them worse and even cause them to occur. Learning that nothing terrible was going to happen and that she could reduce the intensity and duration of the attack through breathing and "grounding," Marissa became less fearful of the panic attacks. This also helped allay the fear that others would see her anxiety. Between sessions, she practiced slow, even breathing at the first sign of building anxiety. Grounding let her shift her attention off the physical sensations and racing thoughts that she experienced during a panic attack by focusing on her surroundings or a particular object. Armed with these strategies, Marissa continued going into situations that had become "triggers" for her panic attacks: the exposure component of her treatment. Success with these strategies would confirm Marissa's new beliefs that she could manage the panic attacks.

Strong empirical evidence has proven that a combination of psychotherapeutic medication and cognitive-behavioral therapy (CBT) is the most effective treatment for most anxiety disorders. Other types of psychotherapies, such as interpersonal therapy, may be useful in conjunction with these two major approaches. Some people present to their primary care physician (PCP) with complaints of anxiety symptoms. The PCP may recommend one or both of the aforementioned approaches. Many PCPs will provide medication initially if the case is straightforward; however, if there is a complicated clinical picture or if there are multiple diagnoses, the PCP may refer the patient to a psychiatrist. Other people with anxiety disorders might begin their treatment journey by consulting a private psychiatrist, a therapist, or a behavioral health clinic. The initial assessment of the patient should indicate whether the disorder is severe enough to warrant treatment with medication. Some patients choose to forego medication and try CBT first. The treating therapist will then refer the patient for a medication evaluation if the anxiety is too overwhelming to allow full engagement in the therapy.

In my private practice, I have found that medication generally reduces the intensity of anxiety symptoms but does not eliminate them. However, on occasion, medication can completely eradicate anxiety symptoms. When it does, patients are less likely to engage in the work of learning anxiety-management strategies. Even if they do engage in the therapy, the strategies are less likely to be effective when patients have not had the experience of actually mastering their symptoms. When there is complete relief of symptoms, I have worked in conjunction with the patient and the psychiatrist to reduce the medication dosage so that there is some experience of anxiety to allow for mastery of the CBT skills and "retraining" the brain. This is significant because the CBT work is essential to long-term progress, whereas medication is more useful in the short term.

## PSYCHOPHARMACOLOGY

Five classes of medications have been found to be effective in reducing the symptoms of anxiety: anxiolytics (benzodiazepines and azapirones), antidepressants (tricyclics, SSRIs, and serotonin-norepinephrine reuptake inhibitors [SNRIs]), beta blockers, antipsychotics, and anticonvulsants (e.g., gabapentin).

All of these medications relieve anxiety, but they are used for different purposes or with different types of patients.

In the treatment of most anxiety disorders, the first-line psychopharmacological intervention is usually the prescription of an SSRI, such as fluoxetine (Prozac), sertraline (Zoloft), paroxetine (Paxil), fluvoxamine (Luvox), citalopram (Celexa), or escitalopram (Lexapro). The patient is started at a low dose of the medication, which is then increased in gradual steps to a therapeutic level. This approach lets the patient adjust to the medication and allows the patient and the physician to judge its effectiveness. Generally, SSRIs take four to six weeks to begin to reduce symptoms. Patients may experience some transitory side effects, such as fatigue, insomnia, and stomach upset, which last for the first two to three weeks. Additional side effects of SSRIs may include joint and muscle pain, diarrhea, jitteriness, and changes in sexual responsiveness. The physician will most likely switch to another SSRI if the medication is not effective or well tolerated. These medications are sometimes not effective at all for some patients. The next option is to change to a different type of drug, such as an SNRI (e.g., venlafaxine [Effexor]), a tricyclic antidepressant, or an anticonvulsant.

All the antidepressants carry a "black box warning" that alerts physicians and patients to the finding that there may be an increase in suicidal thinking and behavior in children, adolescents, and young adults during the first one to two months of treatment. Black box warnings are the U.S. Food and Drug Administration's (FDA's) system of communicating alerts to prescribing physicians when research findings raise a concern about patient safety. The warnings are placed on the drug information sheets surrounded by a bold black box.

There is controversy about the research findings that prompted the placement of the black box warnings on antidepressants. For example, in looking at suicidality in patients on these medications, one must remember that depressed patients have a high incidence of suicidal thinking and behavior. It may be difficult to decipher drug ineffectiveness versus drug-induced suicidality versus coincidental suicidality as the cause of "increased" suicidal thinking and behavior. Another possible artifact is that the drug may improve some patients' energy enough that they begin to act on suicidal thoughts that are already present. It certainly does not hurt to have physicians and patients become more vigilant about suicidality in conjunction with these medications; however, the harm is in the reluctance to use these medications when true benefit may be gained.

There is concern about a life-threatening condition called serotonin syndrome that can happen when SSRIs, SNRIs, and medicines used to treat migraine headaches known as triptans are used together. Serotonin syndrome involves serious changes in brain, muscle, and digestive system functioning due to high levels of serotonin in the body.

### Disorder-Specific Recommendations

Research, often due to pharmaceutical companies' agendas, has sometimes focused on specific medications for specific anxiety disorders. For example, there was much early evidence supporting the use of Luvox for the treatment of obsessive-compulsive disorder (OCD). Subsequent research has indicated that other SSRIs are equally beneficial. In some cases, however, specific medications do appear to be more effective than others for a certain disorder. Other anxiety disorders do not seem to respond well to medication. Specific phobia is one such disorder that does not appear to benefit from psychopharmacological interventions. In fact, the use of a benzodiazepine or SSRI tends to interfere with the effect of exposure-based treatment and increases the likelihood of relapse.

There has been some use of SSRIs to treat posttraumatic stress disorder (PTSD), but the empirical evidence is not impressive. The strongest support has been for the use of Zoloft, which has now received FDA approval for use with PTSD. Behavioral and CBT approaches have been much more effective in treating PTSD.

Anxiolytics, specifically benzodiazepines, can be used initially to treat severe panic disorder, social phobia, and generalized anxiety disorder (GAD) in conjunction with an SSRI. Commonly used benzodiazepines include diazepam (Valium), alprazolam (Xanax), lorazepam (Ativan), and clonazepam (Klonopin). Because they are fast acting, benzodiazepines provide relief from the intensity of symptoms until an SSRI can reach a therapeutic level. This short-term use of a benzodiazepine can enable the patient to begin CBT. However, long-term benzodiazepine use tends to interfere with the effectiveness of CBT treatment. In addition, research evidence points to increased risk of relapse and medication dependency if benzodiazepines are used long-term. Benzodiazepines are especially contraindicated in patients who have alcohol problems or are in recovery from alcoholism. Both substances are central nervous system depressants and, therefore, behave synergistically; that is, they combine to increase the sedating effect. Benzodiazepines are as addictive as alcohol for the recovering person.

Azapirone is another type of anxiolytic that is useful for treating GAD. The most frequently used and most effective azapirone is buspirone (Buspar), which is slower acting than benzodiazepines (it can take up to two weeks to be effective), does not cause sedation, and does not seem to have dependence potential. Buspar also seems to help alleviate co-occurring depression. Common side effects include dizziness, headaches, nervousness, diarrhea, and sweating.

Certain drugs do target particular disorders fairly well. For example, the tricyclic antidepressant clomipramine (Anafranil) is fairly effective in treating OCD, and the monoamine oxidase inhibitor (MAOI) phenelzine (Nardil) has been shown to be effective with social phobia. These drugs are no longer first-line psychotropic treatments since the newer drugs are better tolerated by patients and are often even more effective. Tricyclics and MAOIs are sometimes used to augment the newer medications in patients who have not been responsive to other medication.

Beta-blockers, whose primary function is to reduce blood pressure, have been used since the 1970s to treat the symptoms of performance anxiety (social phobia). They operate to block the physiological symptoms of anxiety and thus prevent the anxiety from interfering with performance. When used as needed, they are effective for symptom control. An example of a beta-blocker is the drug propranolol (Inderal). A survey of more than two thousand professional musicians found that 27 percent of them used beta-blockers to manage stage fright. Seventy percent of these musicians obtained the medication without a physician's prescription.

On occasion, atypical antipsychotic medications are used to treat severe anxiety disorders, especially refractory, or treatment-resistant, OCD. These medications include risperidone (Risperdal), quetiapine (Seroquel), olanzapine (Zyprexa), and aripiprazole (Abilify). Common side effects of these medications include transitory sedation, headache, insomnia, vivid dreams, agitation, dry mouth, weight gain, and constipation. In the past, other antipsychotic medications were used in low doses to manage anxiety, but the side effects from these medications were often devastating, and the sedation was too great.

As mentioned earlier, the anticonvulsant medication gabapentin has shown some effectiveness with anxiety and is sometimes used when other first-line medications are ineffective. This conclusion has largely been drawn from case studies and open trials, meaning the physicians knew that they were prescribing gabapentin and therefore could not control for bias in their studies. Double-blind studies, in which prescriber and evaluator do not know whether the subjects have been given the drug in question or a placebo, are necessary for FDA approval. Completed double-blind studies have not been as supportive for the use of gabapentin in the treatment of anxiety disorders, other than for social anxiety.

## PSYCHOTHERAPY

As already mentioned, the preferred psychotherapeutic treatment approach for anxiety disorders is CBT. The form of CBT used today has been developed by numerous research therapists, including Joseph Wolpe, Donald Meichenbaum, Albert Ellis, Aaron Beck, David Burns, David Barlow, Richard Heimberg, Edna Foa, Judith Rapaport, and Terrence Keane.

### The Theory behind CBT

Building on the thinking and research of Charles Darwin, George Kelly, and Jean Piaget, Beck proposed that it is in an individual's early and continued experiences that schemata (or schemas) are developed. Schemata are cognitive structures or constructs, as Kelly called them, that help us process information and allow us to make ongoing sense of our world without having to encounter each event as a totally new experience. In most cases, these schemata are very adaptive. Unfortunately, if a person develops faulty schemata, all sorts of trouble can ensue. If I believe that I must always get A grades in the courses I take, I might become very anxious and feel pressured to always perform perfectly on assignments and exams. I will then behave in a manner that I think will ensure that I achieve perfect scores, perhaps by staying up all night to study, forgoing food and leisure activities, and becoming irritable if I think I haven't done enough. In addition, I will be devastated if I fail to achieve my unrealistic goals.

A predisposition to certain disorders, such as anxiety or depression, will help determine how schemata are constructed; in other words, how events are interpreted and what assumptions are made. Having the genetic propensity toward anxiety, an individual will likely develop many threat-laden schemata and cognitions. It naturally follows that the individual would frequently experience anxiety and behave accordingly. Faulty schemata are maintained in place because they provide short-term rewards. For example, if a person avoids flying (the behavior) because of a distorted belief that air travel is unsafe, he or she never has to experience the anxiety of confronting this belief. Cognitive therapy helps the individual identify erroneous or distorted cognitions and then challenge them through reasoning, logic, and evidence to restructure these beliefs to be more realistic. The rational response that is generated is then used as the person reenters the anxiety-provoking situation again and again until mastery is accomplished.

### Techniques

The fundamental objective of CBT is to identify and challenge one's distorted thinking. Beck and others have designed a systematic way to proceed with this task. The therapist assists the patient in identifying the automatic thoughts and underlying beliefs (schemata) that are associated with an anxious response to a situation. The next step is to challenge the thoughts and beliefs by examining such things as alternative explanations and evidence for and against the belief. The patient is led through this process by using a thought record, which provides columns for the situation, emotion, automatic thoughts, evidence for and against, and finally the rational response, which will be an alternative or modified thought. The thought record provided by Greenberger and Padesky in *Mind over Mood* (1995) is a particularly useful version of this tool. It has practical questions that lead the patient through the steps. Following the generation of rational responses, the person then must systematically apply them to the situation in question. The new cognitions may also be accompanied by techniques, such as diaphragmatic breathing, to address the physiological symptoms of anxiety. Practice and repetition will hopefully lead to a shift in thinking that will have an impact on the emotional (anxious) response. The process essentially retrains the brain.

This cognitive restructuring underpins much of CBT treatment. Numerous other techniques that incorporate more behavioral components can also be used depending on the presenting picture and specific anxiety disorder. A crucial behavioral component in CBT is relaxation training. Edith Jacobsen's progressive muscle relaxation is a widely used strategy. It consists of progressively tensing and relaxing muscle groups from head to toe and focusing on breathing in concert with the tension and release. Breathing has been discovered to be key in the management of anxiety symptoms. Slow, deep, rhythmic diaphragmatic breathing is a way to access the parasympathetic system and begin a chain reaction of physiological calming. It is a primary component in the treatment of panic attacks and is useful for any experience of anxiety.

As mentioned earlier, Meichenbaum's systematic desensitization is important in its own right and is also the foundation for other types of exposure-based techniques. Coupled with cognitive restructuring, it is particularly useful in the treatment of specific phobias and PTSD. Variations of systematic desensitization are valuable in the treatment of social phobia, panic disorder, and GAD. The steps of systematic desensitization are as follows:

1. Teach the patient progressive relaxation.
2. Construct an anxiety hierarchy related to the stimulus (e.g., a mental image of a dog, a photograph of a dog, seeing a dog across the street, and so on until the final step of actually petting a dog). Develop a relaxing mental image.
3. Using the relaxation technique and its image, introduce gradual exposure to the stimulus utilizing the hierarchy. After a step is mastered (i.e., no anxiety with the presentation of the stimulus), move on to the next step.

An outgrowth of systematic desensitization is exposure treatment, which is a fundamental component in the treatment of many anxiety disorders. The concept is to utilize cognitive restructuring and expose the patient to progressively more difficult aspects of the frightening situation. It is used with specific phobias, PTSD, social phobia, panic disorder, and OCD. PTSD treatment may involve either in vivo exposure, such as returning to the site of the traumatic event, or imaginal exposure. Imaginal exposure is used when returning to the original site is impractical or impossible, such as with childhood abuse. It involves using the cognitive and breathing skills while imaging the feared situation. The goals in exposure treatment are the elimination of avoidance and the mastery of the situation.

In dealing with OCD, the treatment of choice is the combination of medication and the exposure-response prevention (ERP) technique. Symptoms of OCD do not respond to cognitive restructuring and relaxation. Instead, it seems the curative factor is the experiencing of the anxiety and habituating or getting used to the stimulus. The patient encounters the feared stimulus, the ritual is not performed, and he or she "sits with" the anxiety until it diminishes on its own (habituation). Sitting with the anxiety requires that the person not distract himself or herself, use relaxation strategies, or seek reassurance. This is an extremely unpleasant approach. As my teacher in OCD treatment, Dr. Steven Willis, put it, "It would be like sticking your hand in a bucket full of snakes and forcing yourself to keep it there." The therapist is inviting the patient to induce the anxiety that he or she is desperately trying to avoid or reduce. If the issue of motivation is not addressed, many people will not do the ERP work and may drop out of treatment altogether. It has been my experience that it is essential to help the patient make a commitment to do this difficult work by emphasizing the ultimate relief and the ability to regain one's life. The person also has to believe that this treatment will work. Establishing the therapy as a collaborative endeavor in which the patient's feedback and input is crucial helps gain commitment as well. The strategy of developing a hierarchy of OCD situations in which the patient can begin with the least-threatening situation also aids with compliance and provides reinforcement as mastery is gained. ERP is a very powerful tool when it is used consistently.

## FAMILY INVOLVEMENT IN TREATMENT

Education about the patient's disorder is important for family members, as it increases understanding and helps alleviate some of the frustration of living with a person with an anxiety disorder. Whenever possible, it is crucial to include family members in the treatment of panic disorder, PTSD, and OCD. Often, parents or partners have learned to accommodate the patient's anxiety by being a "safe person" who accompanies the agoraphobic patient on outings or abides by the rules of the patient's OCD. Changing the accommodating behavior is collaboratively addressed and incorporated into the patient's hierarchy of situations. In the treatment of children, a parent can function as a coach to ensure that ERPs are being performed. It is also important that parents not punish OCD behaviors or force anxious children into situations for which they are not prepared. Partners of people with anxiety disorders, in their frustration, may become critical and angry and may need support of their own. Either occasional involvement in the identified patient's treatment or a separate referral for treatment may be appropriate.

## ADDITIONAL INTERVENTIONS

Eye movement desensitization and reprocessing (EMDR) was discovered by chance and pioneered by Francine Shapiro in the late 1980s. It is a technique that seems to have some supporting empirical evidence in the treatment of PTSD, although the exact mechanism of action is unknown. Distressing thoughts, images, and emotions seem to be altered in the process of administering EMDR. It has been shown to be at least as effective as the best treatment approaches. EMDR has many components, including the soliciting of trauma-related images and memories, evaluation of the psychological and physiological reactions to the recollections of the event(s), cognitive assessment and restructuring, and repeated lateral eye movements while the patient is focusing on the traumatic response or the modified cognitive appraisal. Because so many components of EMDR are shared in common with the other treatment methods for PTSD, it is difficult to decipher whether the eye movement component has any added value. Thus far, research findings have not supported the claim that it does. In addition, EMDR is not supported by an underlying theoretical framework. More research is required on this particular treatment strategy.

A psychosurgical technique has been found to be effective in treating some cases of refractory OCD. In the 1950s, an alternative was developed to the disappointing psychosurgery technique known as lobotomy. Bilateral stereotactic cingulotomy involves severing fibers in the anterior cingulate gyrus, a small fold in the brain connecting the limbic system, which deals with emotions such as fear, and the frontal lobes, whose functions include judgment and reasoning. An electrode or gamma knife that focuses beams of radiation is guided to the target area by means of a process known as stereotactic magnetic resonance imaging. A small lesion is created there to sever the supracallosal fibers of the cingulum bundle. The anterior cingulate gyrus plays a role in cognitive and attentional control. In a study completed in 2002 at Massachusetts General Hospital, approximately 45 percent of patients previously unresponsive to medication and CBT interventions for OCD were at least partly improved after cingulotomy.

## CASE EXAMPLES IN TREATMENT

The subsequent examples, which follow some of the cases presented earlier, illustrate common treatment regimens for the presenting illnesses.

### Aubrey's Story

Aubrey began treatment for GAD by relating her symptoms to her obstetrician/gynecologist, who prescribed Paxil and also referred her to a psychologist for CBT treatment. After learning about the nature of GAD and the course of treatment, Aubrey began to identify the automatic thoughts related to her anxiety by focusing on an event of the previous week. Aubrey and the psychologist worked on her thought record together. This yielded the following:

**Situation:** Aubrey's husband was uncharacteristically late returning from work and had not called her.

**Emotion:** Anxiety

**Automatic Thoughts:** "I just know he's been in an accident—he always calls if he's late! How will I find out where he is? He's probably dead. Oh what will we do? How can I raise this baby by myself? What will we do for money? We'll lose the house. I can't go back to work with the baby, my parents can't help us—they have health problems. I can't bear to lose him—I won't be able to go on. I'll be so depressed."

Analysis focused on the primary thoughts (what Greenberger and Padesky call "hot thoughts"), which drove all the other thoughts: "I just know he's been in an accident—he's probably dead." This is an example of "fortune telling," which is one of the several common cognitive distortions identified by Beck and Burns.

### Challenges/Evidence:

**Therapist:** Do you know for sure he's been in accident and is dead?

**Aubrey:** Well, no, but he's seldom late and he always calls.

**Therapist:** Can you think of alternative explanations as to why he might be late?

**Aubrey:** Well, sometimes he has a client meeting that runs over; sometimes the traffic is bad.

**Therapist:** How often does it happen that his meetings run over?

**Aubrey:** Well . . . actually, about once or twice a week.

**Therapist:** So, it seems he's late more often than you remember?

**Aubrey:** Yeah, that's true, but he always calls when he's on his way home.

**Therapist:** Can you think of alternative explanations as to why he didn't call?

**Aubrey:** He might have forgotten his phone, or he might not have finished his meeting yet. Ah . . . he could have gotten a call and wasn't free to call me yet. Hmm, I guess there are a lot of possibilities.

**Therapist:** What actually did happen?

**Aubrey:** He had a meeting with his boss that went really late and because he was in a hurry he left his phone on his desk.

**Rational Response:** "It is much more likely, given past evidence, that he is running late and has not had a chance to call." To be used in similar future situations: "I know that I fortune-tell and I anticipate the worst. It is very likely that an alternative explanation is more accurate, so I will generate alternatives and examine the evidence."

Aubrey continued to do thought records both at home and in sessions and generated new ways of handling uncertainty. She wrote her rational responses on cards to help her learn a new style of thinking about situations. In addition, she began to recognize patterns in her thinking such as the one illustrated in the rational response above. The management of her anxiety improved remarkably.

### The Terror of Contamination

Robin's assessment at the beginning of treatment for OCD included completion of the *Yale-Brown Obsessive-Compulsive Scale* to develop a hierarchy of obsessions and compulsions. Education about the disorder and the treatment was presented. Robin now understood that OCD is a brain disorder and that it is useful to conceptualize that the "OCD-part-of-the-brain" constructs unrealistic rules that the person feels compelled to follow. The patient is then urged to challenge the rules even though this is uncomfortable. (Kids love the idea of breaking the OCD rules.) The therapist made it clear to Robin that treatment was to be collaborative and that her input and feedback were essential. Robin admitted that her practices were excessive, and this was reinforced by the therapist who presented information about the transmission of HIV. Robin began the ERP treatment with the easiest situation on her list. She was instructed to stop washing the doorknobs in her home. When touching a doorknob (without using a glove or a tissue), she was to prevent the ritual of hand washing and rate her level of anxiety using the Subjective Units of Discomfort Scale (SUDS). This scale is a 0-to-10 rating, with 0 being the absence of anxiety or discomfort and 10 being the highest level of anxiety the person has ever experienced with a symptom. Robin was instructed to then focus on the anxiety and her fears around the exposure and not seek reassurance until her SUDS rating dropped in half. This was done in the therapist's office several times and then repeatedly completed as homework. She continued with this item until she was able to touch doorknobs without anxiety, and she then moved on to the next item in her hierarchy.

Progress with the CBT treatment was variable because often Robin did not do the assigned homework. She found it very distressing to consider doing the exposures. Robin, her psychologist, and her psychiatrist conferred, and it was agreed that a new combination of medication would be used to try to reduce her anxiety enough to do the ERP work. The psychiatrist added Anafranil to the Luvox that Robin was already taking. Anafranil is a tricyclic antidepressant with a documented history of alleviating OCD symptoms by itself and also as an augmenting medication. Robin showed only slight improvement, but enough to help her do the exposures. She made good progress with a number of items on her hierarchy and decided to stop taking the medication. Her psychiatrist tapered the medication off until it was completely discontinued. Although Robin experienced an increase in anxiety, she was able to maintain her gains for some time. Additional stress later caused an increase in symptoms, which Robin countered with ERP work, in which she was mildly successful. Robin continues to engage in certain OCD behaviors; for example, she still uses latex gloves to do many activities, but she can purchase groceries without extreme checking or washing and no longer throws items away. Robin will occasionally focus on decreasing her glove use for certain situations, but otherwise chooses to engage in certain rituals, which she refuses to surrender.

### Fear of Embarrassment

Amanda contacted an anxiety disorders clinic that offered group treatment for social phobia. She chose to do the cognitive-behavioral treatment without medication. Amanda was assessed with the *Anxiety Disorders Interview Schedule*, and the ratings for specific social situations varied from moderate to severe, with the situation of a job interview being the most severe. The first group sessions involved education about social phobia and an introduction to the cognitive-behavioral approach to treatment. In addition, relaxation strategies were taught and practiced. Participants shared their stories and, with the help of the group leaders, placed their situations within hierarchies, beginning with the mildest symptoms and proceeding to the most severe. Amanda's hierarchy included, in ascending order, dealing with a store clerk, meeting friends of her friends, returning an item to the store, going to a party with friends, going to a party alone, eating in public, making a presentation, and going on a job interview. Group members were then taught to use thought records and instructed to complete several of them as situations arose over the course of the week. Participants were asked to choose where to begin doing exposures on their hierarchies. Amanda began with her easiest situation, which was talk-ing to a store clerk. A thought record was completed for this specific situation, with the outcome being a final, concise, and easily remembered rational response. She then role-played this situation with the group members using her rational response and relaxation strategies. Amanda was instructed to engage in this interaction in the real world and report back to the group. Once each situation was mastered, she moved through the remaining items in her hierarchy (including eating tacos with the other group members). She reported an absence of anxiety in her milder situations and a significant drop in her anxiety in the more severe situations. A point was made to normalize the experience of anxiety in situations such as public speaking and going on a job interview so that she would not have the unrealistic expectation of ridding herself of all anxiety. Amanda's gains were maintained at six- and twelve-month follow-ups, and she was able to get a job in her field of study.

## TREATMENT SETTINGS

For the most part, anxiety disorders are treated on an outpatient basis unless a complicating comorbid diagnosis, such as severe depression or bipolar disorder, warrants inpatient treatment. Today, there are strict criteria for inpatient treatment; specifically, there must be a potential risk of harm to self or others. Several residential treatment programs in the United States treat OCD and PTSD. Being in residence or a partial hospitalization program allows for the intense work required to treat severe OCD and PTSD. A typical residential/partial program provides residence and six-day programming for those who wish to stay at the facility and five-day programming for those who attend the partial hospital program (six to eight hours per day) and live at home. The program is usually one to three months in length. Intensive outpatient programs (IOPs) offer treatment three to five days per week for three to six hours per day. Some programs are offered in the evening so that people can attend and continue to work. All types of anxiety disorders can be treated in an IOP setting. From residential through IOP levels of care, patients are offered group and individual therapy. Exposure therapy, when indicated, is done in both group and individual formats. These programs are staffed by the following personnel: (1) psychiatrists, who evaluate and provide medication; (2) psychologists, who perform psychological and behavioral assessments and guide the behavioral interventions; (3) social workers, who provide family treatment and discharge planning; (4) registered psychiatric nurses, who administer medication and provide counseling; and (5) therapy or behavioral technicians, who manage the milieu (therapeutic community of patients) and provide counseling and behavioral direction. Some programs also offer occupational therapy and art, music, or movement therapy.

Many people with anxiety disorders are treated in outpatient settings where they receive once-a-week therapy from a therapist in a clinic or private practice, and they may also see a psychiatrist or their PCP for medication. Numerous clinic programs offer group therapy on a weekly basis. It is important to assess what level of care is most beneficial for someone and to begin the treatment in the least intensive level of care that seems appropriate. If it becomes clear that the level of care is insufficient, patients should be referred to a higher level of care and then stepped down to a lower level when treatment is successfully completed. For example, a patient may start treatment in an IOP, not respond, and opt to attend a partial hospitalization program. Upon successful completion, the person may be referred to individual therapy, a following psychiatrist, and group therapy once a week.

## RELAPSE PREVENTION

Anxiety disorders are chronic illnesses that must be managed over the lifetime of the patient. A combination of medication and CBT has been proven to provide the best long-term results. The CBT provides a skill set that, if repeatedly practiced by the patient, will ensure consistent gains. The patient must realize that life transitions, stressors, physical illnesses, medications, physical maturation, and aging can trigger new episodes of anxiety disorders and possibly mood disorders. Relapse prevention must be taught as a component of the treatment. Patients must practice anxiety management strategies during treatment so that they can access these skills on an ongoing basis. When the disease recurs, the interventions should begin immediately before the symptoms become unmanageable. Many therapists encourage patients to return to therapy when necessary for a "tune-up." Chronic anxiety disorders can be kept at controllable levels if the patient learns management strategies, follows the recommended course of treatment, and has personal and professional support.

Marissa attended weekly therapy for sixteen weeks and saw Dr. Neville once a month. Dr. Hamilton encouraged her to continue to do exposures armed with her new strategies and cognitive arguments. With persistence, Marissa began to see significant changes in her experience of panic attacks. They became less frequent, and when they did occur, they were never as bad as they had been initially. Dr. Hamilton and Marissa discussed how periods of stress in Marissa's life might bring on the panic attacks again but that now she had a way of coping. They also did some work around stress management.

Marissa decided to get back into jogging, paid better attention to getting enough sleep, and made sure to take breaks and have some fun, but she was cautioned not to rely on alcohol to provide relief. Dr. Neville discontinued the Ativan as Marissa developed mastery with the CBT strategies. After sixteen weeks of therapy, Marissa and Dr. Hamilton met every other week, and eventually they met monthly to make sure Marissa's progress was sustained. Marissa continued to take the Zoloft, with the plan to consider discontinuing its use following the next summer.

# 8

## Future Directions

Human beings have attempted to make sense of our mental and emotional life and mental illness for centuries. We are bound by our style of scientific inquiry, philosophy, spiritual frame of reference, cultural biases, and technology. These factors have determined how we have defined anxiety disorders through time. We have tried to explain anxiety disorders and other mental illness with various theories: demonic possession, physical anomalies, nerve problems, personal weakness, and brain dysfunction. Physicians, scientists, and philosophers have wrestled with ways to make sense of and cure or alleviate anxiety for centuries. There were hints of insight along the way. The Greeks figured it out best without the technology to truly examine their theories. At a fundamental level, they understood the role of the brain and the nervous system. Unfortunately, these theories were lost for centuries, as the technology to provide the supporting evidence was not yet developed.

Great advances were made in the latter half of the twentieth century. Research in the 1990s, in particular, propelled us forward, during what was designated the Decade of the Brain. Technological advances allowed great leaps in our understanding of brain anatomy, neurocircuitry, and neurochemicals, and they raised even more new questions. Technology changes rapidly,

## The Decade of the Brain

In 1990, President George H.W. Bush designated the 1990s the Decade of the Brain, "to enhance public awareness of the benefits to be derived from brain research" through "appropriate programs, ceremonies, and activities." The National Institute of Mental Health and the Library of Congress endeavored to advance the goals set forth in the president's proclamation. Research, educational activities, and conferences were initiated and funded to expand exploration and to acquaint both the general public and lawmakers with cutting-edge research on the brain (http://www.loc.gov/loc/brain/).

and it is staggering to imagine the discoveries ahead of us. Advances in science hold great promise for our ability to make even greater strides.

## CLASSIFICATION

As mentioned earlier, there is an ever-evolving attempt to improve the classification of mental disorders, including anxiety disorders. Current classification issues regarding anxiety disorders include the investigation of biological and genetic determinants and differences in treatment outcome that may aid in differentiating subtypes of disorders. The ultimate goal of improving classification is to enhance treatment efficacy.

Researchers are attempting to tease out differences in obsessive-compulsive disorder (OCD) symptoms and what are called OCD spectrum disorders. The symptom of hoarding has been classified under OCD since it clearly involves obsessions and compulsions. Hoarding occasionally occurs with other OCD symptoms, but is usually the predominant and often the solitary symptom. The manifestations range from collecting newspapers and magazines, food items, old bills, and bank statements to taking in large numbers of animals. The symptom of hoarding does not respond to treatment with medication and is very resistant to exposure-response prevention (ERP) strategies. Genetic studies have indicated a distinct feature on chromosome 14 that is unique to hoarders. In addition, a positron emission tomography (PET) imaging study conducted at the Neuropsychiatric Institute of the University of California, Los Angeles (UCLA), has discovered that the brain activity of patients with hoarding compulsions differs from those with other OCD symptoms. This finding will hopefully lead to the development of different medications that could improve treatment success for patients who hoard.

Hoarding appears to be differentiated from other OCD symptoms, and many of its sufferers tend to be more impaired than those with nonhoarding OCD. Furthermore, the hoarding of animals has components that distinguish it from typical hoarding and OCD. People who suffer from this type of hoarding are predominantly female, over sixty years of age, and unmarried, and more than half of sufferers live alone. Animal control authorities often discover that there are numerous dead animals in the home and that the animals are neglected and living in filth. The patient generally insists that the animals are well maintained and is unable to acknowledge the dire conditions. Treatment is seldom effective, and the recidivism rate is very high. Research is indicating that general hoarding and animal hoarding should be either subcategories of OCD or identified as distinct disorders. More research is called for to explore distinguishing characteristics and to propose improved treatment regimens.

The OCD spectrum disorders include obsessive-compulsive personality disorder (the presence of OCD traits without intense anxiety and impairment); tic disorders, such as Tourette's disorder (the presence of vocal and motor tics); hypochondria (preoccupation with having a serious disease); trichotillomania (hair pulling and skin picking); body dysmorphic disorder (having the fixed belief that an aspect of one's appearance is grossly flawed and trying compulsively to hide or alter that aspect); and, some would suggest, eating disorders. Patients who suffer from these spectrum disorders often also meet the criteria for OCD, but these disorders are not classified as anxiety disorders. Researchers are exploring their relationship to OCD and reexamining their classification.

The various circumstances under which someone develops posttraumatic stress disorder (PTSD) are also being examined for possible subtyping and characterization. Prolonged, ongoing trauma, as in the case of long-term refugee status and ongoing child abuse or sexual molestation, creates a different stress pattern than a one-time event. Patients suffering from complex PTSD experience unique symptoms. The survivor may feel responsible for the abuse, can be preoccupied with the perpetrator and his or her alleged power, and may seek revenge. In addition, those who suffer from chronic traumatic experiences sometimes have severe problems with affect regulation, where emotional responses are uncontrollable and unpredictable, and often resort to self-harm or self-mutilation as a way to cope with distressing affect. Frequently, survivors of chronic abuse are diagnosed with a personality disorder such as borderline, dependent, or histrionic personality, and there is a tendency to blame the victim. From the borderline personality disorder (BPD) frame of reference, it has been observed that many patients with BPD have a trauma history. Again, further knowledge about this phenomenon will aid in the development of effective treatment.

## ETIOLOGY AND BIOLOGY

Of all the anxiety disorders, PTSD had been the least researched disorder until recent years. Fortunately, the wealth of research currently being conducted has revealed much about this complex disorder and its contributing etiological factors. For example, women are twice as likely to develop PTSD as men, and it has been observed that African Americans and Hispanic Americans are more likely to develop PTSD than European Americans. This was identified even after taking into account or controlling for the fact that, in the United States, these former groups are exposed to more traumatic events. No clear answers exist as to why women and members of the above racial and ethnic groups are more vulnerable to the development of PTSD. Many questions need to be answered regarding PTSD and resilience, constitutional factors, and the role of environment and family. The goal of research is to improve prediction and enhance the ability to develop hardiness or resistance to PTSD, especially for members of the military.

### Genetics

The study of genetics holds much promise for the ability to predict, treat, and hopefully alter the development of anxiety disorders. Recognizing that people who have a genetic predisposition to anxiety disorders are more easily triggered by stress to experience impairing anxiety, Finnish researcher Iiris Hovatta and colleagues focus their work on trying to understand the molecular and cellular processes that link genes to the regulation of anxiety behavior. In a study published in 2008, Hovatta's team found that specific genes correlated with specific anxiety disorders, including generalized anxiety disorder (GAD), social phobia, and panic disorder. Further work is necessary to replicate these findings and support this research, but the outlook is promising. Already, collaborators in Spain and the United States are attempting to replicate these findings to see whether the genes identified by Hovatta's group also predispose other populations to anxiety disorders.

As mentioned earlier, there are interesting findings around the catechol-O-methyltransferase gene (see Chapter 5). Again, replication is important, as is further research on the exact action of the enzyme produced and its impact on the neurotransmitters in the prefrontal cortex.

### Neurobiology

Some of our knowledge about neurotransmitters has come from studies focused on the function of the drugs used to treat anxiety disorders. This area still holds promise as research continues. An interesting example of this is a result of the 1977 discovery of benzodiazepine receptors in the brain, which led to the conclusion that the naturally occurring substance in the brain that binds to these receptors may be anxiolytic. These substances have yet to be discovered. The discovery that selective serotonin reuptake inhibitors (SSRIs) seem to stimulate the growth of serotonin-specific neurons leads to further research on the exact mechanism of how the brain creates and utilizes serotonin in response to SSRI treatment.

Promising results from studies that have examined the neurobiological correlates of therapeutic improvement have emerged. Early studies have shown improved autonomic nervous system functioning, specifically improved parasympathetic tone, following cognitive-behavioral therapy (CBT). Jeffrey Schwartz has reported brain activity changes observed via neuroimaging following CBT treatment of OCD. Neuroimaging has allowed for the identification of the brain structures that are implicated in the experience of anxiety disorders. A PET scan, in which a radioactive isotope is attached to glucose, is used to identify active parts of the brain when the patient is introduced to particular stimuli. A useful example of this is the identification of brain structures involved in OCD. In 1994, it was observed that there is a loop of electrical activity from the frontal lobe to the basal ganglia and back to the frontal lobe, seemingly creating a "stuckness" that is characteristic of OCD. This was discovered to be altered by the administration of Prozac. The use of PET scans and other neuroimaging techniques will lead to further discoveries about the functioning of the brain in anxiety disorders.

## TREATMENT

### Psychopharmacology

A better understanding of the genetics and the biological processes of anxiety disorders will likely improve and expand their treatment options. No specific pharmaceutical solutions are currently available for anxiety, since benzodiazepines are not an answer and the antidepressants that are prescribed for the treatment of anxiety disorders are not effective for all patients. Researchers have noticed significant differences among SSRI nonresponders. For example, for some patients, SSRIs do not boost the availability of serotonin, while other patients may experience an increase in available serotonin but it is not utilized by the receptor sites. Scientists are investigating the causes of these failures and possible solutions. Deeper understanding of neurobiology will aid in the development of better drugs specifically targeting anxiety disorders.

In 2006, pregabalin (Lyrica), a medication that had been approved for the management of neuropathic (nerve) pain and seizures, was approved in Europe for the treatment of GAD. Lyrica was approved following five randomized double-blind clinical trials involving more than two thousand patients, with significant findings of efficacy in managing emotional and physical symptoms of anxiety. A paper presented at the annual conference of the American Psychiatric Association in 2009 reported promising results, especially with refractory anxiety disorders. Lyrica is believed to calm extra electrical signals in the nerves, thus reducing nerve pain, and also calming the increased neural excitability of anxiety. Further research is needed for U.S. Food and Drug Administration (FDA) approval of Lyrica in the United States. In addition, studying the mechanism of action of Lyrica may lead to increased understanding of the neural workings of anxiety disorders.

In the case of PTSD, there has been minimal support for pharmacological interventions. As mentioned, Zoloft has some support and received FDA approval for PTSD management. In addition, Prozac has shown some efficacy in the treatment of women with PTSD. Psychopharmacological treatment of PTSD is still in its early stages, and attention needs to be focused on the various presentations of the disorder. Studies continue to develop new pharmaceuticals and to examine combined treatments for PTSD.

Specific phobias seldom respond to pharmacological treatment, and if they do, the medication tends to interfere with CBT treatment. However, there may be certain types of specific phobias with similarities to panic with agoraphobia, such as the fears of driving and flying, and claustrophobia, which may benefit from the use of an SSRI. Further research is needed to explore the viability of such treatment.

### Other Biological Treatments

Eye movement desensitization and reprocessing (EMDR) is being used in the treatment of PTSD, and evidence has shown that it is possibly as effective as exposure and cognitive strategies, but not better. It is usually coupled with other treatment approaches, which makes the outcome of EMDR difficult to separate from the other components of treatment. Since there are no psychological or cognitive neuroscience theories behind EMDR, basic research must be done to determine the neurological changes that allegedly take place and to determine whether it is a treatment component with any real value.

The psychosurgical intervention of bilateral cingulotomy for the treatment of OCD was discussed earlier, but there are also some early favorable results for other neurosurgical treatments. Deep brain stimulation (DBS), which was developed in Europe in the late 1980s and first used in the United States at the Mayo Clinic, stimulates the brain with mild electrical signals, causing the brain's electrical impulses to be reorganized. This has been used to treat essential tremor and Parkinson's disease since 1997. A battery-operated pulse generator is implanted near the collarbone and is attached via a subcutaneous (under the skin) wire to an insulated wire lead with four electrodes at the tip, which is surgically implanted into the targeted area of the brain. The generator is left on during waking hours and sends electrical impulses to the brain. The most common side effects, which are mild and reversible, are a temporary tingling in the limbs, slight paralysis, slurred speech, and loss of balance. Although the surgery is risky, patients tolerate the treatment well and have a significantly improved quality of life.

Scientists have observed that DBS also reduces depressive and obsessive-compulsive symptoms, and as a result, studies have focused on the use of DBS to treat these mental disorders. A modified device has been designed to target OCD, since the areas of the brain that are affected are different from those for movement symptoms. A study by Helen Mayberg of Emory University in 2005 identified the particular area to be targeted in the subgenual cingulate region of the brain. The device was approved for the treatment of severe, refractory OCD in early 2009. Unfortunately, the surgical procedure carries some risks, but the results have been dramatic. Subjects for this study, led by Benjamin Greenberger at Brown University, were severely impaired by their OCD, and most have been restored to a reasonable level of functioning in their lives, including returning to work. Research continues, and this technique could eventually replace cingulotomy as a treatment for refractory OCD.

## Naturopathic Treatment of Anxiety Disorders

Alternative medicine attempts to address medical illnesses with a combination of natural therapies in order to restore balance and normal bodily functioning. This approach has a very strong mind-body emphasis. Since the daily functioning of people affects their well-being, naturopathic physicians assess nutrition, sleep hygiene, and exercise level, and make adjustments as needed. They also assess the presence of any underlying physical illnesses and treat them accordingly. Numerous strategies exist within the naturopathic realm. Acupuncture falls into this category and has demonstrated some effectiveness in treating anxiety disorders. In addition, natural and synthetic supplements are widely utilized. Vitamins, such as B12 and B-complex, and minerals, such as magnesium, seem to have some effect on anxiety symptoms. Herbal preparations, such as valerian and kava kava, have also been used to treat anxiety disorders. Since these substances are not regulated, their preparations are not standardized. There is very little rigorous study of these applications; however, recognition of their potential usefulness has begun to prompt scientific research. It is also important to assess side effects and any potential for toxicity. The use of kava kava has raised such questions, and it needs to be tested to determine its safety. Naturopathic treatment holds great promise but needs standardization and rigorous study to determine its usefulness and how it might be combined with other approaches to treat anxiety disorders.

### Psychotherapeutic Treatment

The development of CBT was a major leap forward in the treatment of anxiety disorders. Scientists have developed new theories and techniques within this framework and have combined CBT with other psychotherapeutic approaches, including more psychodynamically oriented techniques. Combined methods of psychotherapeutic treatment are especially being studied for the treatment of PTSD. As an adjunctive therapy, interpersonal therapy, which has its roots in psychoanalysis and emphasizes the ways in which a person's relationships and social context maintain symptoms, seems to have efficacy with some people who suffer from PTSD. Much treatment-outcome research focuses on finding what works best for whom by examining treatment methods designed for particular subpopulations of patients. A variety of factors may affect outcome, such as culture, intelligence, gender, comorbidity, and age. The military itself has taken a huge step forward by establishing programs for returning service people. For example, the U.S. Navy launched weekend workshops for returning personnel in July 2009.

Research is also focusing on early intervention and prevention of anxiety disorders. Learning about protective factors and parenting styles assists in designing these types of programs for children. For example, identifying children with behavioral inhibition or anxiety sensitivity can prompt a referral for early intervention. Research has shown a significant long-term reduction in anxiety in children with anxiety traits (anxious, but not yet meeting criteria for a specific diagnosis), separation anxiety, and social phobia who were treated in a school-based program. Programs are also being developed that can be family-based and include parent training. Some schools already have programs to help children deal with bullying, which is a risk for shy, inhibited children. It would be interesting to do longitudinal studies of children who have received early intervention treatment to examine the course of the illness over time and utilization rates of later therapy. Studies also have looked at the best years for early intervention. Some findings indicate that the best time for intervention appears to be in middle childhood. Much more exploration in the area of early intervention and prevention within a developmental model is needed.

### Mindfulness Meditation

Ancient approaches cultivated in Asia, such as the practice of yoga, have provided people with ways to manage anxiety and stress for eons. Western medicine has discovered and come to value these strategies, along with a growing acceptance of the mind-body connection. Scientific study has confirmed the beliefs that such techniques can affect physiological functions, such as heart rate, blood pressure, brain function, endocrine function, the immune system, and healing.

Medical researcher Jon Kabat-Zinn has incorporated a particular type of mindfulness and yoga practice into an eight-week intensive training program in mindfulness-based stress reduction (MBSR), in which participants learn mindfulness meditation. Kabat-Zinn is the founding director of the Stress Reduction Clinic and the Center for Mindfulness in Medicine, Health Care, and Society at the University of Massachusetts Medical School. He put this protocol to empirical test and found that many benefits were gained for health, well-being, anxiety symptoms, and stress management. His work has focused on the role that mindfulness meditation can play in health-related areas, such as chronic pain, stress-related disorders, anxiety, panic, chronic diseases, breast cancer, and healing processes. Kabat-Zinn also has applied this practice to societal, workplace, and organizational issues. Through his work, which spans more than thirty years, he has brought a practice that existed largely in the spiritual realm into modern medical science. The use of MBSR has become so widespread that one can log on to the Web site of the University of Massachusetts Medical School Center for Mindfulness and find hundreds of programs offered within the United States and internationally. The University of Pittsburgh Medical Center, for example, offers both MBSR training and a focused MBSR training for those who suffer from anxiety disorders.

According to Kabat-Zinn, "mindfulness is a way of learning to relate directly to whatever is happening in your life, a way of taking charge of your life, a way of doing something for yourself that no one else can do for you—consciously and systematically working with your own stress, pain, illness, and the challenges and demands of everyday life" (from Center for Mindfulness Web site). An essential component of mindfulness is the concept of acceptance, which leads to the ability to "relate directly to whatever is happening" rather than struggle against reality or dwell on catastrophic possible outcomes. Mindfulness helps a person stay in the moment rather than ruminate about the past and worry about the future. This type of mental stance is crucial in the management of anxiety and is consistent with the goals of CBT for treating anxiety.

Studies conducted by Kabat-Zinn, Philippe Goldin at Stanford University, and other researchers have shown the effectiveness of MBSR in the reduction of symptoms in patients suffering from GAD, panic disorder, and social phobia. Goldin's research, funded by the National Institutes of Health, utilizing neuro-imaging is focused on how meditation affects the brain. He is investigating cognitive-affective mechanisms in healthy adults and those suffering from psychopathology. Goldin is specifically examining the neurological effects of mindfulness meditation and CBT on emotional reactivity, as well as emotional and attention regulation. In addition, he is studying the effect of mindfulness meditation training on parents and children and their family interactions, compassion, and anxiety. This approach may have utility in early intervention.

### The Incorporation of Mindfulness in Psychotherapeutic Approaches

Because of the success of MBSR and some preliminary findings that it is a useful adjunct to psychotherapy, there is a trend toward incorporating either components of mindfulness or the full mindfulness meditation into traditional forms of therapy, especially CBT and behavioral therapy. Marsha Linehan, a research psychologist who has developed a very effective therapy for those with borderline personality disorder (BPD), incorporated mindfulness into a treatment method that grew out of CBT called dialectical behavior therapy (DBT). Since many people who carry a diagnosis of BPD have suffered chronic trauma and exhibit symptoms of the proposed diagnostic category of complex PTSD, her findings have great significance for the treatment of PTSD. A major focus of DBT is learning mindfulness and other skills to improve affect regulation, which is a predominant symptom of complex PTSD.

Schwartz, a research psychiatrist at UCLA, incorporated mindfulness into his four-step method for the treatment of OCD. Still using an ERP format, he adds the steps of being mindful and accepting the OCD thoughts for what they are. In other words, Schwartz advocates relabeling the thoughts as OCD and reattributing them to the result of brain malfunction by acknowledging that OCD is a medical illness. Schwartz recommends that the patient, while preventing the compulsive ritual, then refocus and shift attention and activity to something else. The final step consolidates the prior three in revaluing the OCD thoughts and feelings as meaningless and strengthening the ability to challenge the OCD thoughts the next time they arise.

The four-step approach runs counter to the theory behind the traditional ERP strategy of taking the OCD at face value ("Yes, I will contract HIV because I touched that doorknob") and focusing on the fear and anxiety induced by the response prevention until habituation (natural reduction in anxiety) occurs. Proponents of traditional ERP would critique the refocus step as avoidance behavior, therefore robbing the ERP of its real brain-changing power. Schwartz and colleagues present evidence via neuroimaging techniques, however, that brain activity actually changes as a result of the four-step/ERP interventions. More research needs to be done to compare Schwartz's approach with traditional ERP treatment and determine the most active ingredients in the therapeutic approaches.

Schwartz's colleagues at UCLA have broadened the incorporation of mindfulness into mindfulness-based behavior therapy, which addresses other anxiety disorders and mental disorders. Mindfulness-based cognitive therapy (MBCT) was developed by Zindel Segal, Mark Williams, and John Teasdale and was based on Kabat-Zinn's MBSR program. MBCT originally focused on the treatment of depression and has had significant success in this area. Preliminary data on the use of MBCT in the treatment of GAD and panic disorder have been promising. Randomized controlled studies are the next step in the discovery of MBCT's usefulness with these anxiety disorders.

### Rethinking an Accepted Treatment Component for Panic Disorder

Controlled breathing has long been recognized as an effective treatment component for panic disorder. Slow, deep breathing can trigger the parasympathetic nervous system to bring about a calming physiological response. This has been proven to be especially useful when the patient's panic symptoms include hyperventilation. On the other hand, studies have also shown that breathing retraining does not appear to have any independent value, since patients can learn to manage their panic attacks with cognitive restructuring and exposure alone. Some researchers are currently questioning the role of controlled breathing and consider it more as a distraction or avoidance of dealing with the panic symptoms. This viewpoint categorizes breathing retraining as a safety behavior and proposes that it detracts from the power of the exposure. David Barlow and colleagues, who had been proponents of breathing retraining, now discourage its use in treatment except when the patient clearly hyperventilates.

### A FINAL NOTE

All this research and development ultimately matters to the practicing clinician and the patients being treated. Ongoing research is currently examining various components of treatment, which should lead us to further refine and develop our psychotherapeutic and pharmacological approaches. A strong emphasis on treatment-outcome research and quality improvement has led to the development of standardized practices and "pathways of care." Pathways of care are developed and utilized in hospitals and clinics and prescribe each step of assessment, intervention, and discharge planning. The American Psychiatric Association has published practice guidelines, which it updates as research findings warrant. These guidelines are specific to the *Diagnostic and Statistical Manual* diagnoses and cover assessment, treatment planning, education, evaluation of treatment progress, levels of care, and a summary of research findings regarding epidemiology, natural history and course of the illness, and genetic and family studies. In addition to these practice guidelines being available for practitioners, training programs for mental health professionals and professional trade organizations such as the American Psychiatric Association and the American Psychological Association strongly encourage the use of evidence-based treatment protocols.

In addition to psychotherapy research, neuroscience plus pharmaceutical and genetic research will lead the way to new and improved methods of bringing relief to the millions of people who suffer from anxiety disorders. The National Institute of Mental Health strongly supports and funds brain imaging studies using such technologies as PET scanning and functional magnetic resonance imaging, which have revolutionized human brain research. As we refine these technologies further, we will discover patterns of connectivity in the human brain and will be able to observe changes in neurotransmitter systems that occur when people are under stress and when they are treated. We are on the brink of a new era of exploration, since we have ever-evolving technology with which to enlighten us. However, we must never lose the human touch of our treatment approaches. The early-twentieth-century method of the Weir Mitchell cure, forced feeding with milk aside, led physicians to recognize the importance of the one-to-one relationship of the clinician and patient in treating mental disorders. No matter what technological advances bring us, we must always keep the clinician-patient relationship central to treatment.

# Timeline

**ca. 100,000 years ago: The Paleolithic Era:** Evidence has been found of trephining and the use of amulets to relieve mental disorders and ward off the spirits that caused them. Animistic theories are current: these are the belief that animated forces of nature act upon the human mind and soul, resulting in odd behaviors.

**ca. 6000–4000 BCE:** Taoism and acupuncture are alleged to have their roots in China's New Stone Age. Opium is discovered to be mood-altering and is used to relieve pain and reduce stress.

**ca. 3000 BCE:** Yoga is developed in India.

**2750 BCE:** Earliest known record of an explanation for mental illness from ancient Babylon: caused by deities angered by sinful behavior.

**ca. 2000 BCE:** Koyak and Wiros tribal warriors in Russia use mind-altering substances to reduce fear and increase endurance.

**3000–500 BCE: Babylonian, Egyptian, and Ancient Greek Civilizations:** Mythological theories: angry gods are seen as the cause of mental maladies in disobedient individuals.

The Greek god Pan is seen as the cause of fear and anxiety—that is, panic. Priests, shamans, and medicine men treat mental disorders.

**ca. 1300 BCE:** In China, headaches and other "head disorders" are believed to be caused by the "malevolent agencies of the wind."

**ca. 700 BCE:** The Chinese *Kuan Tzu* states that there are institutions for the treatment of the insane.

**652–588 BCE:** The Greek scholar Thales states that human behavior can be explained by underlying scientific principles.

**ca. 600–500 BCE:** Observations of strategies to deal with fear and anxiety in warfare are noted by Greek writers.

**582–510 BCE:** Pythagoras refines and promotes the idea of the need for a balance of humors for good mental health. He is the first to identify the brain as the seat of rationality and, consequently, mental dysfunction.

**557–491 BCE:** Alcmaeon dissects the brain and central nervous system. He combines the humoral theory with the knowledge of the nervous system.

**509 BCE–325 CE: The Roman Empire:** Practice of humane treatment of the mentally ill.

**500–332 BCE: The Greek Classical Age:** The move away from spiritual explanations for human behavior begins. Temples are established in the Greek countryside for those with physical and mental illnesses. Diet, rest, comfort, massage, music, and the use of sedative drugs are the key components used for a return to health. Exorcism and punishment as curatives for mental illness are denounced by Greek philosopher-scientists.

**470–399 BCE:** Socrates promotes self-analysis and insight as a path to mental health. "Know thyself" was his directive to followers.

**460–367 BCE:** Hippocrates writes case studies on depression and phobia. He proposes that anxieties, dread, and fears originate from an imbalanced brain and emphasizes empirical studies to uncover knowledge. Hippocrates and colleagues develop a classification system for the mental disorders. They identify hysteria and phobias. Diagnosis becomes the basis for treatment.

**429–347 BCE:** Plato identifies erroneous beliefs as the source of many emotions and uses education and rational discussion to alter these beliefs. (This is an anticipation of cognitive therapy.)

**384–322 BCE:** Aristotle makes significant contributions about human learning. He develops the idea of associational linkages (classical conditioning) and the role of reinforcement (operant conditioning) in learning, which are important ideas in the development and maintenance of anxiety, fear, and phobias.

**ca. 300 BCE:** The Chinese *Shan Hai Ching* lists twenty drugs used to treat anger, fear, and jealousy.

**30–90 CE:** Aretaeus examines premorbid (prior to illness) conditions that make patients vulnerable to mental illness and studies the long-term course of mental disorders.

**131–201:** Galen develops the study of neuroanatomy. He holds to humoral theories and the influence of animal spirits (a common Roman belief). He compiles and interprets the Greek and Roman accumulated medical knowledge and refines the classification of mental disorders. He identifies anxious depression and obsessionality.

**255–320:** Aurelianus begins a regressive movement embracing spiritual explanations for mental illness.

**ca. 300:** The disintegration of the Roman Empire also heralds a decline in science and the humanitarian treatment of the mentally ill. Christianity promotes the concept of demonic possession as a cause of aberrant behaviors and mental illness. The works of the Greek philosophers are banned and condemned.

**354–430:** Aurelius Augustine (St. Augustine) attempts to reintroduce Greek thinking and reconcile it with Christianity.

**ca. 476–1000: Fall of Rome and the Beginning of the Dark Ages:** There is a return to spiritual explanations and treatment for mental disorders. Fueled by the chaos of the times and the Roman Catholic Church's attempt to establish control and order, demonological theories become more prevalent. Inhumane treatment of the mentally ill returns.

**870–925:** Najab ud-din Unhammad identifies nine categories of mental illness, including "lovesickness" with anxiety and depression, and anxious and ruminative states of doubt (obsessions and compulsions).

**980–1037:** Avicenna and Ishaq ibn Amram acknowledge anxiety symptoms as part of depression (melancholy). Avicenna considers exaggerated fearfulness to be a personality trait.

**1135–1204:** Maimonides works to reconcile classical Greek writing with Jewish and Islamic law.

**1200s:** Albert Magnus (1193–1280), Roger Bacon (1214–1292), and Thomas Aquinas (1225–1274) promote the work of the Greek and Roman philosophers and scholars.

**1300–1600: The Renaissance:** Universities flourish, and the classical Greek and Roman writings are rediscovered and taught. Art, science, medicine, and rational philosophy advance dramatically.

**1527:** Paracelsus introduces laudanum, a mixture of alcohol and an opium derivative.

**ca. 1600:** The use of water spas to cure a variety of ills grows significantly.

**1596–1650:** René Descartes develops the notion of mind-body dualism: that the body and mind have the ability to influence each other.

**1621:** Robert Burton publishes *Anatomy of Melancholy*, in which he describes obsessive-compulsive disorder (OCD) and is one of the first to distinguish "madness" from anxiety and melancholy. He recommends that people share their sadness or worry with a sympathetic listener.

**1664:** Thomas Willis is the founder of biological psychiatry and publishes *Cerebri Anatome*, detailing studies of the brain and nervous system, which he terms "neurology," and studies of the mind, which he terms "psychology." He believes mental disorders are related to the nervous system, not humors. Willis proposes that hysteria is a nervous disorder.

**1624–1689:** Thomas Sydenham, who values empirical research, conceptualizes the etiology of mental disorders as arising from both organic and environmental/temperamental causes.

**1680:** Sydenham concocts his own form of laudanum to relieve stress and nervousness.

**Mid-1700s:** George Cheyne publishes *The English Malady*, proposes that hysteria and other neurotic ailments are a disorder of the nerves, and promotes the practice of "nerve doctors." William Cullen and Robert Whytt support this notion and identify the "neuroses."

**1775–1783: The American Revolution**

**Late 1700s:** Franz Anton Mesmer, later followed by James Braid, develops the technique of hypnotism and the modern conceptualization of the unconscious.

**1789–1799: The French Revolution**

**1826:** Bromide salts are discovered to help induce sleep and calm the nerves.

**1832:** Chloral hydrate is synthesized and sold to relieve anxiety and induce sleep.

**Mid-1800s:** Jean-Martin Charcot, Paul Briquet, and Ernst von Feuchtersleben identify disorders that are distinct from hysteria, thereby narrowing its definition. The mentally ill are still treated in asylums, but there is a shift toward identifying nervous problems and treating the nervous at spas and in private medical practices.

**1856–1926:** Emil Kraepelin collects detailed case studies and puts together a taxonomy of mental disorders that serves as the basis for our modern classification system. He distinguishes the emotional disorders, which include the anxiety disorders, from more severe mental illness. He distinguishes psychogenic from physiological origins for mental disorders.

**1864:** Adolf von Baeyer develops barbituric acid, which is used to treat anxiety and insomnia.

**1872:** Charles Darwin publishes *The Expression of Emotion in Man and Animals* and concludes that fear and anxiety serve a survival function. His work serves as a catalyst for the study of emotion.

**1879:** Wilhelm Wundt establishes the first experimental psychology department at the University of Leipzig.

**Late 1800s:** George Beard identifies "neurasthenia" or "tired nerves" and Silas Weir Mitchell develops his "rest cure," which stimulates interest in the curative factors of the patient-physician relationship. Sigmund Freud and Josef Breuer, using hypnosis with hysterical patients, develop the idea of repressed emotions and the need for their release. This fuels Freud's development of psychoanalytic theory.

**1898:** The Bayer Company commercially releases Heinrich Dreser's new drug, Heroin.

**Early 1900s:** Ivan Pavlov discovers classical conditioning, and Edward Thorndike lays out the principles of operant conditioning. This launches the study of learning and behavioral psychology. The practice of psychoanalysis is widespread and popular.

**1913:** John Watson publishes "Psychology as the Behaviorist Views It" in *Psychology Review,* proposing that all of human behavior can be explained by learning principles.

**1914–1919: World War I**

**1920:** The "Little Albert" experiments are conducted by Watson and Rosalie Rayner, showing the development of a learned fear response.

**1920s:** Walter Cannon's work in physiology begins to identify brain structures and the action of nerve cells that explain emotional responses.

**1924:** Mary Cover Jones uses learning principles to extinguish a learned fear response, beginning the use of behavioral principles in the treatment of anxiety.

**Early to mid-1900s:** Behavioral psychology gains credibility and support from the research and theorizing of B.F. Skinner, O.H. Mowrer, and others. Other components involved in learning are added to behavioral theory by Edward Chase Tolman and by John Dollard and Neal Miller, who incorporate the concepts of cognition, social and cultural learning, and the unconscious.

**1941–1945: World War II**

**Mid-1900s:** Joseph Wolpe and Hans Eysenck independently propose that an innate physiological vulnerability and experiences explain the development of anxiety disorders.

**1952:** Betty Tworag identifies the neurotransmitter serotonin. From earlier work by Henri Laborit and Pierre Deniker, chlorpromazine is sold in the United States as Thorazine, the first antipsychotic drug. Low doses of antipsychotics are used to treat anxiety.

**1955:** George Kelly publishes his personal construct theory, which lays the groundwork for the development of cognitive-behavioral therapy (CBT). Albert Ellis develops and publishes his early work on rational emotive therapy.

**1955:** Meprobamate (Miltown), an anti-anxiety drug, is presented to the psychiatric community, and its use becomes widespread.

**1957:** Arvid Carlsson identifies the neurotransmitter dopamine. The first antidepressant, iproniasid (Marsilid), is developed and marketed.

**1958:** Wolpe publishes his work on systematic desensitization.

**1960:** Imipramine (Tofranil) is the first tricyclic antidepressant to be developed. It changes serotonin levels and is discovered to alleviate anxiety symptoms. The first benzodiazepine, chlordiazepoxide (Librium), is released.

**1962:** Stanley Schachter and Jerome Singer's landmark study on cognitive appraisal is published.

**1967:** Aaron Beck publishes a book on depression and its treatment and introduces cognitive therapy. He goes on to further develop CBT to address anxiety disorders.

**1971:** Arnold Lazarus publishes *Behavior Therapy and Beyond*, which outlines a form of CBT.

**1980s:** Research on emotion advances. CBT is empirically validated as the treatment of choice for anxiety disorders. David Barlow does groundbreaking research on the treatment of panic disorder.

**1983:** The first edition of the *Anxiety Disorders Interview Schedule* is published by Barlow and colleagues.

**1987:** Fluoxetine (Prozac), the first selective serotonin reuptake inhibitor, is marketed.

**1990s:** President George H.W. Bush declares this to be the "Decade of the Brain." Specific CBT approaches are refined for specific anxiety disorders, especially posttraumatic stress disorder.

**1990s–2000s:** Technological advances in neuroscience lead to new discoveries about the workings of the brain and nervous system.

**1994:** Jon Kabat-Zinn publishes *Where Ever You Go, There You Are* and outlines his work on mindfulness meditation, which later is integrated with CBT.

**1997:** Deep brain stimulation (DBS) is used to treat essential tremor; it will be discovered to alleviate OCD symptoms.

**1998:** Jeffrey Schwartz and Lewis Baxter's work using positron emission tomography (PET) scans with patients with OCD is published, showing brain changes in response to treatment.

**2000:** Eric Kandel and Arvid Carlsson receive the Nobel Prize for their work on learning and brain function.

**2008:** Iiris Hovatta and colleagues discover specific genes that correlate with specific anxiety disorders, including generalized anxiety disorder, social phobia, and panic disorder.

**2009:** A DBS device for the treatment of OCD is approved for use.

# Glossary

**Agoraphobia:** The avoidance or fear of being out in public, usually accompanied by the fear that one might experience an anxiety or panic attack and not be able to escape.

**Alienist (*archaic*):** A term used in the latter part of the nineteenth century, meaning psychiatrist. It comes from the French *aliene*, meaning insane, and was used in reference to "mental alienation," or loss of mental faculties.

**Amygdala:** A small, almond-shaped structure in the limbic system of the brain that is responsible for alerting the organism to a threat.

**Analogue:** A chemical compound that resembles another substance in its molecular structure. For example, gabapentin is an analogue of gamma-aminobutyric acid (GABA).

**Augment:** To add to.

**Autonomic nervous system (ANS):** Part of the peripheral nervous system that is responsible for the functioning of organ (visceral) processes. It controls involuntary muscles and comprises three parts: the sympathetic, parasympathetic, and enteric nervous systems (see below).

**Basal ganglia:** A group of neuron bundles located at the base of the forebrain that is involved with involuntary movement, motor control, coordination, cognition, speech, and learning. This collection of neurons connects the cerebral cortex, thalamus, and limbic system and seems to be involved in obsessive-compulsive disorder and Tourette's and tic disorders.

**Baseline:** Measurement taken at initial assessment or in a study before any intervention is applied. It is the standard for the subject against which change is measured.

**Central nervous system (CNS):** The brain and spinal cord.

**Cerebral cortex:** The thin outer layer of the brain, called grey matter, which is composed of nerve cells and nerve pathways. The cerebral cortex is responsible for higher brain functions such as thought, perception, advanced motor function, social abilities, language, problem solving, and memory.

**Cingulate gyrus:** A structure of the limbic system that coordinates sensory input with emotions. It provides a pathway from the thalamus (which lies between the cerebral cortex and the midbrain structures of the limbic system) to the hippocampus and seems to be responsible for focusing attention on emotionally significant events. It is implicated in obsessive-compulsive disorder (OCD) and is the target of the surgical technique of cingulotomy in the treatment of OCD.

**Classical conditioning:** A process of learning by which a subject comes to respond in a desired manner to a previously neutral stimulus that has been repeatedly presented along with an unconditioned stimulus that elicits the desired response. Pavlov presented dogs with what he called an unconditioned stimulus, i.e., food. The stimulus of food elicits salivation, which is an innate, automatic response, or in Pavlov's terms, an unconditioned (not learned) response. He then paired the food with the ringing of a bell (conditioned stimulus) and found that the dogs would salivate to the ringing of the bell prior to, or even without, the presentation of the food. He labeled this a learned or conditioned response. Pavlov further investigated the fate of a conditioned response when the conditioned stimulus, which in this case was the bell, is removed. He discovered that after several such trials (food with no bell) the conditioned response gradually stopped, or extinguished.

**Contraindicated:** A condition that makes a particular treatment inadvisable.

**Corticotropin-releasing hormone (CRH):** A hormone produced and released by the hypothalamus, which acts on the pituitary gland to release adrenocorticotropic hormone (ACTH, also known as corticotropin), which in turn stimulates the release of cortisol. Part of the hypothalamic-pituitary-adrenocortical axis, CRH is implicated in the neurophysiology of anxiety disorders.

**Cortisol:** A hormone that is released by the adrenal gland when the sympathetic nervous system is activated to assist in the fight-or-flight response. In turn, it is reduced by the parasympathetic nervous system. With chronic stress or trauma, cortisol levels remain high and affect the body in negative ways.

**Diaphragmatic breathing:** Breathing with conscious full utilization of the diaphragm muscle, which is located below the ribs and above the stomach. It involves pushing the diaphragm downward as one inhales (the stomach will move outward with the inhalation) and allowing the diaphragm to return to its resting position with the exhalation. This is an important anxiety management tool.

**Electroencephalogram (EEG):** A means of studying electrical activity in the brain. Electrodes are placed on the head that are able to read the electrical impulses in the brain and record them in a graphical format.

**Empirical:** Relying on observation or experiment to draw conclusions.

**Endocrine system:** Through a system of glands, the endocrine system releases hormones that influence bodily processes such as growth, metabolism, mood, sexual function, and reproduction. The endocrine system and the nervous system work together closely to help the body function properly.

**Enteric nervous system (ENS):** Part of the autonomic nervous system that regulates the digestive system. It has connections to the sympathetic, parasympathetic, and central nervous systems.

**Epidemiology:** The study of the occurrence, distribution, and control of diseases within a population.

**Etiology:** The study of the causes and origins of diseases.

**Frontal lobe:** The cerebrum contains five lobes in each hemisphere. The frontal lobe is the largest of the five and is responsible for "executive functioning," which involves planning, recognition of consequences, decision making, judgment, long-term memory, and conceptualizing.

**Gamma-aminobutyric acid (GABA):** An amino acid that functions as the major inhibitory neurotransmitter in the central nervous system. It decreases the excitatory activity of neurons and has been found to increase benzodiazepine binding to receptor sites, thereby inducing relaxation.

**Habituate:** In behavior modification, to lose responsiveness to a particular stimulus, to get used to a stimulus.

**Hippocampus:** A long, curved ridge, shaped like a seahorse, that underlies each lateral ventricle in the brain. It is part of the limbic system and is responsible for memory formation, storage, and processing.

**Homeostasis:** The tendency of the body to maintain a state of balance through physiological feedback loops.

**Humors (*archaic*):** The substances in the body allegedly responsible for personality and temperament; when out of balance, they were held to be responsible for mental and physical disorders. The humors were associated with the four elements of water, fire, earth, and air. An overabundance of the water humor tended to produce too much phlegm and caused a victim to be apathetic and lethargic. Air was associated with blood and created optimism. (We describe a person as "sanguine" who is cheerfully confident and optimistic. The root of the word "sanguine" comes from the Latin *sanguineus*, meaning "of blood.") The earth humor created black bile, which could bring on depression, melancholy, and anger if not in proper balance. Too much fire and yellow bile would result in excessive irritability. An innate preponderance of one humor over the others would create a personality type, and an imbalance of humors was believed to cause mental or physical illness.

**Hyperglycemia:** A condition in which there is an abnormally high level of glucose in the blood.

**Hypervigilance:** A state of constant scanning of the environment for threats to one's safety.

**Hypochondriasis:** A psychiatric condition in which patients are continuously convinced that they suffer from a physical illness despite evidence to the contrary.

**Hypothalamic-pituitary-adrenocortical (HPA) axis:** A system of interactions and feedback loops that influence the neuroendocrine system in response to stress through the release of a glucocorticoid, which in humans is cortisol. The HPA axis affects the immune system, energy levels, and metabolism.

**Hypothalamus:** A structure in the limbic system that regulates hunger, thirst, and responses to pain, pleasure, sexual stimuli, fear, anger, and aggression. The hypothalamus is responsible for endocrine function and is connected to the pituitary gland, which in turn releases hormones into the bloodstream and affects the rest of the endocrine system and the parasympathetic and sympathetic nervous systems.

**Hysteria (*archaic*):** First designated by the Greeks, it was a condition believed to be caused by a "wandering uterus" or sexual frustration. Allegedly affecting women for the most part, its symptoms included fatigue, nervousness, irritability, insomnia, emotionality, and a "tendency to cause trouble." Over the years, other symptoms were added, causes shifted, other illnesses were found to explain the symptoms (including anxiety disorders), and eventually the label was dropped.

**Irritable bowel syndrome (IBS):** A disorder of the large intestine that causes diarrhea and constipation, sometimes in an alternating pattern, and abdominal cramping, bloating, and gas. IBS is aggravated by anxiety and stress. It can be controlled by diet and stress management.

**Limbic system:** A system located in the midbrain and composed of several structures, including the hippocampus, hypothalamus, cingulate gyrus, and the amygdala. The limbic structures are important in the regulation of visceral motor activity, emotional expression, and responses to threat.

**Locus ceruleus:** A small area in the brainstem consisting of a pair of identical nuclei (clusters of neurons) connecting the cerebral cortex and the limbic system. It is a major center that produces and regulates norepinephrine, which in turn activates the autonomic nervous system. The locus ceruleus is involved in the physiological response to stress and danger.

**Mental status exam (MSE):** A structured interview that is part of a comprehensive psychological or psychiatric assessment that gathers information about a patient's mental functioning.

**Milieu:** A therapeutic community of patients, for example, in an inpatient or partial hospital program.

**Neurasthenia (*archaic*):** The term given by physician George Beard in the 1800s to describe a physical illness centered in the nerves. The symptoms were similar to those of hysteria and included fatigue, aches and pains, nervousness, weakness, loss of appetite and weight, and diminished memory. A subclassification of this diagnosis is defined today as chronic fatigue syndrome.

**Neurotransmitters:** Chemical messengers that enable neurons (nerve cells) to pass signals from one to another. Electrical signals trigger the release of these chemicals at the synapse (the space between two neurons). Neurotransmitters play an important role in the development of brain disorders and in their treatment. Examples are serotonin, dopamine, and norepinephrine.

**Norepinephrine (noradrenaline):** A catecholamine neurotransmitter produced by the adrenal glands that stimulates the sympathetic nervous system.

**Obsessions:** Persistent, intrusive thoughts, impulses, or images.

**Operant conditioning:** Learning that occurs when the frequency of a behavior is either increased or decreased because of the results of the behavior (positive or negative reinforcement or punishment).

**Orbital frontal cortex (OFC):** The region of the frontal lobe that sits above the orbits of the eyes. It is involved in decision making and is part of the loop of electrical activity observed in patients with obsessive-compulsive disorder.

**Parasympathetic nervous system (PNS):** The part of the autonomic nervous system that is responsible for calming the organism following activation of the sympathetic nervous system.

**Positron emission tomography (PET) scan:** An imaging technique that allows for the locating of electrical activity in the brain. By attaching a radioactive isotope to glucose (the main fuel of the brain), scientists have been able to identify areas of the brain activated during subjects' experience of anxiety.

**Premorbid:** Prior to the onset of an illness.

**Psychogenic:** Originating in the mind or emotions.

**Psychotropic:** Medication that affects the mind, emotions, or behavior.

**Recidivism:** Tendency to repeat criminal behavior.

**Refractory:** Treatment-resistant.

**Reinforcer:** A stimulus that increases a behavior.

**Relapse:** The return of signs and symptoms of a disease.

**Reliability:** Consistency of measurement; the ability of an instrument to yield the same results for the same subject with repeated administration.

**Septohippocampal system:** A structure of fiber connections between the septum (a cortical structure) and the hippocampus of the limbic system. This system is influenced by the neurotransmitters norepinephrine and dopamine and the amygdala. It is involved in the evaluation, categorization, and storage of incoming information relative to reward, punishment, novelty, and nonreward. It is able to compare new stimuli with stored memories of other experiences. It is involved in behavioral inhibition and is thought to be an innate anxiety circuit.

**Serotonin:** A neurotransmitter thought to be implicated in many brain disorders, especially depression and anxiety disorders.

**Serotonin syndrome:** The condition that occurs when high levels of serotonin cause serious changes in the brain, muscles, and digestive system. It can happen when selective serotonin reuptake inhibitors (SSRIs) or serotonin-norepinephrine reuptake inhibitors are used together with medicines used to treat migraine headaches known as 5-hydroxytryptamine receptor agonists (triptans). Signs and symptoms of serotonin syndrome include the following: restlessness, fast heart beat, nausea, diarrhea, hallucinations, coma, and loss of coordination. Serotonin syndrome may be more likely to occur when starting or increasing the dose of an SSRI or a triptan.

**Stereoptypy:** A repetitive or ritualistic movement, such as rocking or hand flapping.

**Subcutaneous:** Under the skin.

**Sympathetic nervous system (SNS):** The part of the autonomic nervous system that is responsible for the preparation of the organism for fight or flight, the response to threat.

**Synergy:** The working together of two or more substances or forces whose outcome is greater than the sum of the parts.

**Taxonomy:** The science of classification.

**Temperament:** Characteristic mode of response; those aspects of personality that are considered innate.

**Thalamus:** A brain structure that relays sensory impulses from the basal ganglia and other parts of the brain to the cerebral cortex and that is involved in associating sensory stimuli and feelings.

**Tourette's disorder:** A neurological disorder in which vocal and motor tics are present. Tics are sudden, repetitive, nonrhythmic motor movements or vocalizations that seem to be outside the control of the patient. Tourette's disorder is considered to be part of the obsessive-compulsive spectrum and frequently co-occurs with obsessive-compulsive symptoms.

**Validity:** The ability of a measurement instrument to actually measure the concept in question.

**Vapors (*archaic*):** Suffering from a nervous condition, hypochondriasis, or depression, supposedly caused by the presence of exhalations within the organs.

**Visceral:** Of the organs.

# Bibliography

American Psychiatric Association. 2000. *Diagnostic and Statistical Manual of Mental Disorders* (4th ed., text revision). Washington, DC: American Psychiatric Association.

Antony, Martin M., and David H. Barlow. 1997. "Social and Specific Phobias." In A. Tasman, J. Kay, and J.A. Leiberman (Eds.) *Psychiatry*. Philadelphia: Saunders.

Argyropoulos, S. V., C. J. Bell, and D. J. Nutt. 2001. "Brain Function in Social Anxiety Disorder." *Psychiatric Clinics of North America* 24(4): 707–722.

Askwith, Richard. 1998. "How Aspirin Turned Hero." *Sunday Times* London: Time Newspapers Ltd., September 13, 1998.

Barloon, Thomas, and Russell Noyes, Jr. 1997. "Charles Darwin and Panic Disorder." *Journal of the American Medical Association* 277(2): 138–141.

Barlow, David H. 2002. *Anxiety and Its Disorders: The Nature and Treatment of Anxiety and Panic* (2nd ed.). New York: Guilford Press.

Barlow, David H., Steven Hayes, and Rosemary Nelson. 1984. *The Scientist Practitioner*. Oxford, United Kingdom: Pergamon.

Barlow, Nora, ed. 1958. *The Autobiography of Charles Darwin 1809–1882*. New York: Norton.

Baxter, Jr., Lewis R. 1991. "PET Studies of Cerebral Function in Major Depression and Obsessive-CompulsiveDisorder: the Emerging Prefrontal Cortex Consensus." Annals of Clinical Psychiatry 3(2): 103–109.

Baxter, Jr., Lewis R., Jeffrey M. Schwartz, Kenneth S. Bergman, Martin P. Szuba, Barry H. Guze, John C. Mazziotta, Adina Alazraki, Carl E. Selin, Huan-Kwang Ferng,

Paul Munford, Michael E. Phelps. 1992. "Caudate Glucose Metabolic Rate Changes With Both Drug and Behavior Therapy for Obsessive-Compulsive Disorder." Archives of General Psychiatry 49(9): 681–689.

Beck, Aaron T., and G. Steer. 1987. *Manual for the Revised Beck Depression Inventory.* San Antonio, TX: Psychological Corporation.

Beck, Judith. 1995. *Cognitive Therapy: Basics and Beyond.* New York: Guilford Press.

Bienvenu, O. Joseph, Jack F. Samuels, Mark A. Riddle, Rudolf Hoehn-Saric, Kung-Yee Liang, Bernadette A. M. Cullen, Marco A. Grados, and Gerald Nestadt. 2000. "The Relationship of Obsessive-Compulsive Disorder to Possible Spectrum Disorders: Results from a Family Study." *Biological Psychiatry* 48(4): 287–293.

Briquet, Paul. 1859. *Traité clinique et thérapeutique de l'hysterie.* Paris: Bailliere.

Brody, Arthur L., Sanjaya Saxena, Jeffrey M. Schwartz, Paula W. Stoessel, Karron Maidment, Michael E. Phelps, and Lewis R. Baxter, Jr. 1998. "FDG-PET Predictors of Response to Behavioral Therapy and Pharmacotherapy in Obsessive Compulsive Disorder." *Psychiatric Research* 84(1): 1–6.

Brown, Timothy, Peter DiNardo, and David H. Barlow. 1994. *Anxiety Disorders Interview Schedule-IV (ADIS-IV).* New York: Oxford University Press.

Burns, David D. 1981 (revised and updated, 1999). *Feeling Good: The New Mood Therapy.* New York: William Morrow and Co.

Burns, David D. 1984. *Intimate Connections.* New York: William Morrow and Co.

Burns, David D. 1989 (revised and updated, 1999). *The Feeling Good Handbook.* New York: William Morrow and Co.

Burns, David D. 2007. *When Panic Attacks: The New, Drug-Free Anxiety Therapy That Can Change Your Life.* New York: Random House.

Burton, Robert. 1621. *Anatomy of Melancholy: What It Is.* Oxford, England: John James Lichfield for Henry Short Cripps.

Cannon, Walter B. 1915 (2nd edition, 1929). *Bodily Changes in Pain, Hunger, Fear, and Rage.* New York: D. Appleton & Co.

Cannon, Walter B. 1923. *Traumatic Shock.* New York and London: D. Appleton & Co.

Christmas, David, Colin Morrison, Muftah S. Eljamel, and Keith Matthews. 2004. "Neurosurgery for Mental Disorders." *Advances in Psychiatric Treatment* 10: 189–199.

Comer, Ronald J. 2009. *Abnormal Psychology* (7th ed.). New York: Worth Publishing.

Comrie, J. D. 1922. *Selected Works of Thomas Sydenham.* London: Bale Sons & Danielson.

Craske, Michelle G., David H. Barlow, and Elizabeth A. Meadows. 2000. *Mastery of Your Anxiety and Panic: Therapist Guide for Anxiety, Panic, and Agoraphobia (MAP-3).* (Fear and Avoidance Hierarchy). San Antonio, TX: Psychological Corporation/Graywind.

Crowe, R. R., R. Noyes, D. L. Pauls, and D. J. Slymen. 1983. "A Family Study of Panic Disorder." *Archives of General Psychiatry* 40: 1065–1069.

Dadds, Mark R., Susan H. Spence, Denise E. Holland, Paula M. Barrett, and Kristin R. Laurens. 1997. "Prevention and Early Intervention for Anxiety Disorders: A Controlled Trial." *Journal of Consulting and Clinical Psychology* 65(4): 627–635.

Darwin, Charles. 1867/1896. *The Expression of Emotion in Man and Animals.* London: J. Murray.

Darwin, F., ed. 1897/2001. *The Life and Letters of Charles Darwin.* Boston: Elibron Classics.

DeGroot, Aldemar, and Dallas Treit. 2004. "Anxiety Is Functionally Separated in the Septo-Hippocampal System." *Brain Research* 1001(1–2): 60–71.

DiNardo, Peter, Timothy Brown, and David Barlow, 1994. *Anxiety Disorders Interview Schedule-IV-Lifetime Version (ADIS-IV-L)*. New York: Oxford University Press.

Donner, Jonas, Sami Pirkola, Kaisa Silander, Laura Kananen, Joseph D. Terwilliger, Jouko Lönnqvist, Leena Peltonen, and Iiris Hovatta. 2008. "An Association Analysis of Murine Anxiety Genes in Humans Implicates Novel Candidate Genes for Anxiety Disorders." *Biological Psychiatry* 21: 672–680.

Ellis, Albert. 1961. *A New Guide to Rational Living*. Cedar Knolls, NJ: Wehman Brothers.

Ellis, Albert. 1998. *How to Control Your Anxiety Before It Controls You*. New York: Citadel Press.

Evans, S., S. Ferrando, M. Findler, C. Stowell, C. Smart, and D. Haglin. 2008. "Mindfulness-Based Cognitive Therapy for Generalized Anxiety Disorder." *Journal of Anxiety Disorders* 22(4): 716–721.

Eysenck, Hans J. (Ed.). 1967. *The Biological Basis of Personality*. Springfield, IL: Charles C. Thomas.

Fava, Maurizio, John Rush, Jonathan E. Alpert, G. K. Balasubramani, Stephen R. Wisniewski, Cheryl N. Carmin, Melanie M. Biggs, Sidney Zisook, Andrew Leuchter, Robert Howland, Diane Warden, and Madhukar H. Trivedi. 2008. "Difference in Treatment Outcome in Outpatients with Anxious Versus Nonanxious Depression: A STAR*D Report." *American Journal of Psychiatry* 10: 1176.

Foa, Edna B., C. V. Dancu, E. A. Hembree, L. H. Jaycox, E. A. Meadows, and G. P. Street. 1999. "The Efficacy of Exposure Therapy, Stress Inoculation Training and Their Combination in Ameliorating PTSD for Female Victims of Assault." *Journal of Consulting and Clinical Psychology* 67: 194–200.

Foa, Edna B., Elizabeth Hembree, and Barbara Olaslov Rothbaum. 2007. *Prolonged Exposure Therapy for PTSD Emotional Processing of Traumatic Experiences: Therapist Guide*. New York: Oxford University Press.

Foa, E. B., D. Riggs, C. V. Dancu, and B. O. Rothbaum, 1993. "Reliability and Validity of a Brief Instrument for Assessing Posttraumatic Stress Disorder." *Journal of Traumatic Stress* 6: 459–474.

Folstein, Marshall F., Susan E. Folstein, and P. R. McHugh. 1975. "Mini-Mental State: A Practical Method For Grading The Cognitive State Of Patients For The Clinician." *Journal of Psychiatric Research* 12(3): 189–98.

Frost, Randy. 2000. "The Hoarding of Animals Research Consortium." *Psychiatric Times* 17: 4.

Gabriel, Richard. 1987. *No More Heroes: Madness and Psychiatry in War*. New York: Hill and Wang.

Goodman, W. K., L. H. Price, S. A. Rasmussen, C. Mazure, P. Delgado, G. R. Heninger, and D. S. Charney. 1989. "The Yale-Brown Obsessive Compulsive Scale: II. Validity." *Archives of General Psychiatry* 46: 1012–1016.

Goodman, W. K., H. Price, S. A. Rasmussen, C. Mazure, R. L. Fleischman, C. L. Hill, G. R. Heninger, and D. S. Charney. 1989. "The Yale-Brown Obsessive Compulsive Scale: I. Development, Use, and Reliability." *Archives of General Psychiatry* 46: 1006–1011.

Greenberger, Dennis, and Christine Padesky. 1995. *Mind Over Mood: Change the Way You Feel by Changing the Way You Think*. New York: Guilford Press.

Hall, Richard C. W., Michael K. Popkin, Richard A. DeVaul, Louis A. Faillace, and Sondra K. Stickney. 1978. "Physical Illness Presenting as Psychiatric Disease." *Archives of General Psychiatry* 35: 1315–1320.

Hamann, Donald L. 1985. "The Other Side of Stage Fright." *Music Educators' Journal* 71(8): 26–28.

Härter, Martin C., Kevin P. Conway, and Kathleen R. Merikangas. 2003. "Associations between Anxiety Disorders and Physical Illness." *European Archives of Psychiatry and Clinical Neuroscience* 253(6): 313–320.

Heimberg, Richard G., Michael R. Liebowitz, Debra A. Hope, and Franklin R. Schneier. 1995. *Social Phobia: Diagnosis, Assessment, and Treatment*. New York: The Guilford Press.

Herman, Judith. 1997. *Trauma and Recovery: The Aftermath of Violence from Domestic Abuse to Political Terror*. New York: Basic Books.

Hippocrates. 1952. "Hippocrates, Galen (Hippocratic Writings / On the Natural Faculties by Galen)." In Adler, Mortimer J., Clifton Fadiman, Philip W. Goetz. *Great Books of the Western World, Vol. 10*. Chicago: Benton.

Hodgson, Barbara. 2001. *In the Arms of Morpheus: The Tragic History of Laudanum, Morphine, and Patent Medicines*. Buffalo, NY: Firefly Books.

Hope, Debra A., and Richard G. Heimberg. 1988. "Public and Private Self-Consciousness and Social Phobia." *Journal of Personality Assessment* 52: 626–639.

Jones, Mary Cover. 1924. "A Laboratory Study of Fear: The Case of Peter." *Pedagogical Seminary* 31: 308–315.

Kabat-Zinn, Jon. 1994. *Wherever You Go, There You Are*. New York: Hyperion Books.

Kandel, Eric R., J. H. Schwartz, and T. M. Jessell (Eds.). 1991. *Principles of Neural Science* (3rd ed.). New York: Elsevier.

Kaplan, Arline. 2007. "Hoarding: Studies Characterize Phenotype, Demonstrate Treatment Efficacy." *Psychiatric Times* 24(6) (http://www.psychiatrictimes.com).

Kendall, Joshua. 2008. *The Man Who Made Lists: Love, Death, Madness and the Creation of Roget's Thesaurus*. New York: G. P. Putnam's Sons, The Penguin Group.

Kendler, Kenneth S., A. C. Heath, N. G. Martin, and L. J. Eaves, 1986. "Symptoms of Anxiety and Depression in a Volunteer Twin Population." *Archives of General Psychiatry* 43: 213–221.

Kendler, Kenneth S., A. C. Heath, N. G. Martin, and L.J. Eaves, 1987. "Symptoms of Anxiety and Symptoms of Depression: Same Genes, Different Environments?" *Archives of General Psychiatry* 44: 451–457.

Kessler, R. C., P. A. Berglund, O. Demler, R. Jin, and E. E. Walters. 2005. "Lifetime Prevalence and Age-of-Onset Distributions of DSM-IV Disorders in the National Comorbidity Survey Replication (NCS-R)." *Archives of General Psychiatry* 62(6): 593–602.

Kessler, R. C., W. T. Chiu, O. Demler, and E. E. Walters. 2005. "Prevalence, Severity, and Comorbidity of Twelve-Month DSM-IV Disorders in the National Comorbidity Survey Replication (NCS-R)." *Archives of General Psychiatry* 62(6): 617–27.

Kessler, R. C., K. A. McGonagle, S. Zhao, C. B. Nelson, M. Hughes, S. Eshleman, H. U. Wittchen, and K. S. Kendler. 1994. "Lifetime and 12-month Prevalence of

DSM-III-R Psychiatric Disorders in the United States: Results from the National Comorbidity Survey." *Archives of General Psychiatry* 51: 8–19.

Kim, Y. W., S. H. Lee, T. K. Choi, S. Y. Suh, B. Kim, C. M. Kim, S. J. Cho, M. J. Kim, K. Yook, M. Ryu, S. K. Song, and K. H. Yook. 2009. "Effectiveness of Mindfulness-Based Cognitive Therapy as an Adjuvant to Pharmacotherapy in Patients with Panic Disorder or Generalized Anxiety Disorder." *Depression and Anxiety* 26(7): 601–606.

Kraepelin, Emil. 1909–1915. *Psychiatri: Ein Lehrbuch* (8th ed., vols. 1–4). Leipzig: Barth.

Lazarus, Arnold A. 1971. *Behavior Therapy and Beyond*. New York: McGraw-Hill.

Liddell, Howard S. 1949. "The Role of Vigilance in the Development of Animal Neurosis." In P. Hoch and J. Zubin (Eds.), *Anxiety*. New York: Grune & Stratton.

Ma, S. H., and J. D. Teasdale. 2004. "Mindfulness-Based Cognitive Therapy for Depression: Replication and Exploration of Differential Relapse Prevention Effects." *Journal of Consulting and Clinical Psychology* 72: 31–40.

Mahone, E. M., M. A. Bruch, and R. G. Heimberg. 1993. "Focus of Attention and Social Anxiety: The Role of Negative Self-Thoughts and Perceived Positive Attributes of the Other." *Cognitive Therapy and Research* 17: 209–224.

Millon, Theodore. 2004. *Masters of the Mind: Exploring the Story of Mental Illness from Ancient Times to the New Millennium*. Hoboken, NJ: John Wiley & Sons, Inc.

Nestadt, Gerald, Anjene Addington, Jack Samuels, Kung-Yee Liang, O. Joseph Bienvenu, Mark Riddle, Marco Grados, Rudolf Hoehn-Saric, and Bernadette Cullen. 2003. "The Identification of OCD-Related Subgroups Based on Comorbidity. *Biological Psychiatry* 53(10): 914–920.

Pearson, Patricia. 2008. *A Brief History of Anxiety: Yours and Mine*. New York: Bloomsbury USA.

*Physician's Desk Reference*. 2008. New York: Thomson Reuters.

Pollack, Mark H., John Matthews, and Erin L. Scott. 1998. "Gabapentin as a Potential Treatment for Anxiety." *American Journal of Psychiatry* 155: 992–993.

Pollack, Mark H., Michael W. Otto, Peter P. Roy-Byrne, Jeremy D. Coplan, Barbara O. Rothbaum, Naomi M. Simon, and Jack M. Gorman. 2008. "Novel Treatment Approaches for Refractory Anxiety Disorders." *Focus* 6(4): 486–495.

Rachman, S. J. 1976. "The Passing of the Two-Stage Theory of Fear and Avoidance: Fresh Possibilities." *Behaviour Research and Therapy* 14: 125–131.

Rachman, S. J., and Peter Muris. 2007. *Normal and Abnormal Fear and Anxiety in Children and Adolescents*. New York: Elsevier.

Roth, Janet H., and Mark R. Dadds. 1999. "Prevention and Early Intervention Strategies for Anxiety Disorders." *Current Opinion in Psychiatry* 12(2): 169–174.

Schachter, S., and J. E. Singer. 1962. "Cognitive, Social, and Physiological Determinants of Emotional State." *Psychological Review* 69(5): 379–399.

Schwartz, Jeffrey M. 1996. *Brain Lock: Free Yourself from Obsessive-Compulsive Behavior*. New York: Harper Collins.

Schwartz, Jeffrey M., and Sharon Begley. 2003. *The Mind and the Brain: Neuroplasticity and the Power of Mental Force*. New York: Harper Collins.

Shorter, Edward. 1997. *A History of Psychiatry: From the Era of the Asylum to the Age of Prozac*. New York: John Wiley & Sons, Inc.

Smoller, J. W., and S. V. Faraone. 2008. "Genetics of Anxiety Disorders: Complexities and Opportunities." *American Journal of Medical Genetics Part C Seminar on Medical Genetics* 148C: 85–88.

Steketee, Gail, J. B. Grayson, and E. B. Foa. 1985. "Obsessive-Compulsive Disorder: The Differences Between Washers and Checkers." *Behaviour Research and Therapy* 23: 197–201.

Stone, Michael H. 1997. *Healing the Mind: A History of Psychiatry from Antiquity to the Present*. New York: W. W. Norton & Company.

Teasdale, J. D., Z. V. Segal, J. M. G. Williams, V. Ridgeway, J. Soulsby, and M. Lau. 2000. "Prevention of Relapse/Recurrence in Major Depression by Mindfulness-Based Cognitive Therapy." *Journal of Consulting and Clinical Psychology* 68: 615–623.

Tolin, David. 2007. *Buried in Treasures: Help for Compulsive Acquiring, Saving, and Hoarding*. New York: Oxford University Press.

Toneatto, T., and L. Nyugen. 2007. "Does Mindfulness Meditation Improve Anxiety and Mood Symptoms? A Review of the Controlled Research." *Canadian Journal of Psychiatry* 52 (4): 260–266.

Torgersen, S. 1983. "Genetic Factors in Anxiety Disorders." *Archives of General Psychiatry* 40: 1085–1089.

Tsigos, C., and G. P. Chrousos. 2002. "Hypothalamic-Pituitary-Adrenal Axis: Neuroendocrine Factors and Stress." *Journal of Psychosomatic Research* 53(4): 865–871.

Watson, John B. 1913. "Psychology as the Behaviorist Views It." *Psychology Review* 20: 158–177.

World Health Organization World Mental Health Survey Consortium. 2004. "Prevalence, Severity, and Unmet Need for Treatment of Mental Disorders in the World Health Organization World Mental Health Surveys." *Journal of the American Medical Association* 291(21): 2581–2590.

Yerkes, Robert M. and Dodson, John D. 1908. "The Relation of Strength of Stimulus to Rapidity of Habit Formation." *Journal of Comparative Neurology and Psychology*. 18: 459–482.

## WEB SITES

American Psychiatric Association. 2010. Practice Guidelines. APA Web Site. http://www.psych.org/MainMenu/PsychiatricPractice/PracticeGuidelines_1.aspx.

American Yoga Association. n.d. General Yoga Information. American Yoga Association Web Site. http://www.americanyogaassociation.org.

Cowell, Adrian. 1998. "The Opium Kings." *Frontline*. PBS Online. http://www.pbs.org/wgbh/pages/frontline/shows/heroin.

Futrell, Shanika L. 2009. Returning Warriors Workshop Offers Sailors, Families Tools for Success. United States Navy Web Site. http://www.navy.mil/search/display.asp?story_id=42108.

Gorbis, Eda, Joseph O'Neill, Jim Sterner, Jenny Yip, and Christine Molnar. 2006. Mindfulness-Based Behavioral Therapy (MBBT) for OCD. Westwood Anxiety Institute/UCLA Web Site. http://www.hope4ocd.com/downloads/OCF2007_MBBT.pdf.

Harvard School of Medicine. 2005. National Comorbidity Survey. Harvard School of Medicine Web Site. http://www.hcp.med.harvard.edu/ncs/.

Lister Hill National Center for Biomedical Communications. 2007. COMT Gene. United States Library of Medicine Web Site. http://ghr.nlm.nih.gov/gene=comt.

Mayo Foundation for Medical Education and Research. n.d. Deep Brain Stimulation. Mayo Clinic Web Site. http://www.mayoclinic.org/deep-brain-stimulation/.

MediLexicon International Ltd. 2006. Pfizer's Lyrica Approved for the Treatment of Generalized Anxiety Disorder (GAD) in Europe. Medical News Today Web Site. http://www.medicalnewstoday.com/articles/40404.php.

National Institute of Mental Health. Last reviewed 2009. NIMH-Funded National Comorbidity Survey Replication (NCS-R) Study: Mental Illness Exacts Heavy Toll, Beginning in Youth. National Institutes of Health Web Site. http://www.nimh.nih.gov/health/topics/statistics/ncsr-study

National Institute of Mental Health. 2008. The Numbers Count: Mental Disorders in America. National Institutes of Health Web Site. http://www.nimh.nih.gov/health/publications/the-numbers-count-mental-disorders-in-america/index.shtml.

Page, Dan. 2004. UCLA PET Study Finds Neurobiology of Hoarders Differs from Other OCD Patients; Findings Open Opportunity for Improving Treatment. UCLA Web Site. http://newsroom.ucla.edu/portal/ucla/UCLA-PET-Study-Finds-Neurobiology-5218.aspx?RelNum=5218.

Pariante, Carmine. 2003. "Depression, Stress, and the Adrenal Axis," Topical Briefings; British Society for Neuroendocrinology. *Journal of Neuroendocrinology* Web Site. http://www.neuroendo.org.uk/content/view/31/11/.

PBS. 1998. A Drug for Treating Schizophrenia Indentified. PBS Online. http://www.pbs.org/wgbh/aso/databank/entries/dh52dr.html.

U.S. Drug Enforcement Administration. n.d. Chloral Hydrate. United States Department of Justice Web Site. http://www.usdoj.gov/dea/concern/chloral hydrate.html.

U.S. Department of Health and Human Services, National Institute of Mental Health. 1992. Epidemiologic Catchment Area Study, 1980–1985. Ann Arbor, MI: Inter-University Consortium for Political and Social Research Web Site. http://www.icpsr.umich.edu/cocoon/ICPSR/STUDY/06153.xml.

University of Massachusetts Center for Mindfulness. n.d. Stress Reduction Program. University of Massachusetts School of Medicine Web Site. http://www.umassmed.edu/Content.aspx?id=41254.

Whealin, Julia M., and Laurie Slone. 2009. Differences between the Effects of Short-Term Trauma and the Effects of Chronic Trauma. National Center for PTSD Fact Sheet. http://www.ncptsd.va.gov/ncmain/ncdocs/fact_shts/fs_complex_ptsd.html.

Yoga Central. n.d. The History of Yoga. The Power of Yoga Web Site. http://www.yoga-central.net.

# Index

## About the Author

**Cheryl Winning Ghinassi** is a psychologist in private practice in Pittsburgh, PA, where she specializes in the treatment of anxiety disorders in children and adults. She graduated with a Ph.D. in Clinical Psychology from the University at Albany, State University of New York. Dr. Ghinassi was formerly a clinical instructor in psychiatry at Harvard Medical School and was the program director for children's inpatient, residential, and partial hospital services at McLean Hospital in Boston.